Melancholia Africana

Creolizing the Canon

Series Editors

Jane Anna Gordon, Associate Professor of Political Science and Africana Studies, University of Connecticut

Neil Roberts, Associate Professor of Africana Studies and Faculty Affiliate in Political Science, Williams College

This series, published in partnership with the Caribbean Philosophical Association, revisits canonical theorists in the humanities and social sciences through the lens of creolization. It offers fresh readings of familiar figures and presents the case for the study of formerly excluded ones.

Titles in the Series

Creolizing Rousseau, edited by Jane Anna Gordon and Neil Roberts

Hegel, Freud and Fanon, by Stefan Bird-Pollan

Theorizing Glissant, edited by John E. Drabinski and Marisa Parham

Journeys in Caribbean Thought: The Paget Henry Reader, edited by Jane Anna Gordon, Lewis R. Gordon, Aaron Kamugisha, and Neil Roberts, with Paget Henry

The Philosophical Treatise of William H. Ferris: Selected Readings from The African Abroad or, His Evolution in Western Civilization, by Tommy J. Curry

Creolizing Hegel, edited by Michael Monahan

Frantz Fanon, Psychiatry and Politics, by Nigel C. Gibson and Roberto Beneduce

Melancholia Africana: The Indispensable Overcoming of the Black Condition, by Nathalie Etoke, translated by Bill Hamlett

Melancholia Africana

The Indispensable Overcoming of the Black Condition

Nathalie Etoke

Translated by Bill Hamlett

ROWMAN & LITTLEFIELD
INTERNATIONAL

London • New York

Published by Rowman & Littlefield International, Ltd.
6 Tinworth Street, London SE11 5AL
www.rowmaninternational.com

Rowman & Littlefield International, Ltd. is an affiliate of
Rowman & Littlefield
4501 Forbes Boulevard, Suite 200, Lanham, Maryland 20706, USA
With additional offices in Boulder, New York, Toronto (Canada), and London (UK)
www.rowman.com

Originally published as *Melancholia Africana: L'indispensable dépassement de la condition noire*, Nathalie Etoke (Editions du Cygne, 2010)

British Library Cataloguing in Publication Information
A catalogue record for this book is available from the British Library

ISBN: HB 978-1-78661-302-8
ISBN: PB 978-1-78661-301-1

Library of Congress Cataloging-in-Publication Data Available

ISBN: 978-1-78661-302-8 (cloth : alk. paper)
ISBN: 978-1-78661-301-1 (pbk. : alk. paper)
ISBN: 978-1-78661-303-5 (electronic)

∞™ The paper used in this publication meets the minimum requirements of American National Standard for Information Sciences—Permanence of Paper for Printed Library Materials, ANSI/NISO Z39.48-1992.

Contents

Series Editors' Note

It has long been an aim of the Caribbean Philosophical Association (CPA) to assure that books that receive our organization's Frantz Fanon Award for Outstanding Book in Caribbean Thought and Nicolás Guillén Award for Outstanding Book in Philosophical Literature be translated into at least one language other than that of the original publication. While our acquisitions editor at Rowman & Littlefield International immediately supported this idea, securing the resources necessary to pay translators to do their indispensable work had, until recently, proved elusive.

Nathalie Etoke's *Melancholia Africana* is the first CPA-sponsored translation of a book that received an association prize.

We wish to thank the Williams College W. Ford Schumann '50 Program in Democratic Studies for providing essential funding to prepare the translation of this work from French into English. We envision the CPA's translation project as a key dimension of the democratizing of global knowledge that we describe as the organization's central purpose of *shifting the geography of reason.*

—Jane Anna Gordon and Neil Roberts
Creolizing the Canon, Series Editors

Foreword

Lewis R. Gordon

Nathalie Etoke's *Melancholia Africana* is here offered in Bill Hamlett's English translation along with LaRose T. Parris's interview with the author. To say that this award-winning book is a testament to Frantz Fanon's famous inaugural work *Black Skin, White Masks* is without exaggeration. It is, after all, the work of a Cameroonian theorist and artist who challenges the boundaries of art, thought, and politics. Like Fanon, her pre-university education was in her homeland and then in France. Unlike Fanon, her homeland is a country in which her Indigenous identity is evident. Also unlike him, she continued her higher education in the United States, in what Fanon once called "a nation of lynchers."

Fanon was not entirely off the mark with his assessment. After all, the United States is the place in which #BlackLivesMatter, the hashtag Alicia Garza posted as a love letter to Black people as police officers and white vigilantes were acquitted one after another for their ongoing slaughter—state-supported lynching. In the title of his study of this phenomenon, the sociologist Noël Cazenave simply called it what it is: *Killing African Americans* (2018). There is an extent to which American national identity, from as far north as Canada to the southern countries of Argentina and Chile, is invested in the ongoing suffering and death of Black people. Its history of settler colonialism offered the same for Indigenous peoples. These are the people who, for the sake of delusions of national integrity and justice, are contradictorily legitimate only when not visible.

Etoke looks into the face of this perverse commitment to not-seeing and not-hearing and draws forth a paradox. Productions of death are also conditions for new forms of life. She, after all, is not only Black but also, in Africa, Indigenous. As she moved from one colonial center to another, the contradictions brought forth reflection, and to all that she examines the contradictions of limited options in the face of existential choice. Even where apparently futile, one must choose, and in doing so encounter, always, what is to be done—or at least a sense of it.

For a theorist, what is to be done is to theorize the situation. Where theorists are rebuked for theorizing is, after all, neurotic where if they abandoned theorizing and took to the streets, complaints would emerge on the absence of reflective understanding of various struggles. For a theorist whose humanity is questioned, however, all theoretical efforts are always saturated with exigency. After all, models of luxury dominate many conceptions of theorists. For those lacking such, their work raises the familiar transcendental reflection: How is such work possible?

This path of making possible what is avowedly impossible—or at least highly improbable—is a task born of what the African American philosopher Leonard Harris calls "philosophy born of struggle." The issue is not one of preconceived notions of what can be done but instead of the urgency about what must be done. That, however, is a calling without guarantees of success. With all actions political—indeed, all actions worthwhile—there is that element of risk. Failure is always the prevailing promise.

An Afro-existential movement that is not in Etoke's mind in these reflections, in light of the challenges of failure, is Afropessimism. The debates in that line of thought often conclude with Black designation as absolute negation. The black, and even the Black, they claim is ontological. And what is this ontological status? All things negative. This means, in effect, that the historical efforts to collapse Black life into death become *faits accomplis*. Etoke's response, without having worked out her argument with this critique in mind, is twofold.

First, she looks into the radicality of death and reminds us of what it means to examine such from points of view outside of the logic of what has become known as "western civilization." In the sub-Saharan communities from which she came, death is part of a continuum that affects actions of the living. Ancestors, from this perspective, live through descendants by virtue of whom they are able to have the identity of ancestors in the first place. This means, then, that the value of becoming ancestors only makes sense in a world committed to descendants. To erase both history and future through a form of fetishized presentism—if it is not *for me*, it loses value—elides other possibilities of action and life. Where death is part of a continuum, it is not exclusively about what others have done. It is what *we* are to do.

I do not think this is an insight exclusive to sub-Saharan peoples and their diaspora. It is there in thought of people across the globe. It has been asphyxiated, however, in the consciousness of many who have taken on the idealized and abstract subjectivity born from the fifteenth-century convergence of Christological notions of purity and Capitalist market fundamentalism whose philosophical anthropology points to racial subjectivity and eventual godlike individualism. The result is a white subject who supposedly depends on nobody, or at least no others, not even the gods and especially not the ancestors. The lie of unaccountability was inevitable, as we now see in a world governed by leaders with no sense of obligation to future life on this planet.

Etoke offers a poem from the African American singer, actor, and poet Jill Scott, a stanza which offers much to consider:

> *Oh, if our ancestors could walk in the dark*
> *Barefoot, afraid in the dark, for miles and miles,*
> *And miles and miles and miles and miles and miles*

I am often asked about my ritual of taking my shoes off when I speak, teach, and eat. My response includes fidelity to the ancestors. We stand on our bare feet before them as custodians of truth. They are witnesses across time, which means, in our willingness to become ancestors, we join a stream of accountability through to descendants. The nakedness of flesh on ground, of standing bare, acknowledges a form of humility born of responsibility. The last point about dining is connected to basic gratitude: we inherit their wisdom for our continued nourishment.

This double symbol of removing in the inauguration of letting go harkens to what, despite the distortion and at times elision of history, must be done. This brings us to the second point. Despite her criticisms of Afrocentrists in this book, she shares with at least those who identify as Africologists—those who study logic and value of practices African and throughout its diaspora in their own right—an important insight: We harm ourselves when we fail to account for ourselves, as African or Black people, as agents of history.

Joining Fanon, Etoke asks at least the theorist to take responsibility for the task of developing new concepts by which to bring forth new and freer modes of life.

Melancholia Africana offers a few such concepts. First, there is the identification of melancholia with which to begin. The term takes on varieties of significance in different genres and approaches to human study. The psychoanalytical one is most prevalent, in which there is the production of a self or subject born of loss. For Black people, the loss is patent. The organizations of power through which Christendom took to the seas and became Modern Europe as a global imperial force brought forth upheavals resulting in the genocide of many Indigenous peoples and the forced enslavement of others. The largest groups kidnapped into forced servitude were sub-Saharans.

People who had no reason to associate their dark complexion with negation were transformed, through brutal processes of commodification and violence, into racially inferior dark peoples alien to their ancestry. They became a new kind of Indigenous people—those born of Euromodernity. That temporal location from which they were born is, however, also one that rejects them. They thus paradoxically belong where they do not belong. This rejected belonging forces onto these subjects an ambivalent relationship to time and possibility. Their past, after all, is one in which they did not exist as a people before colonialism. As rejected in the colonial world they inhabit, there is a form of secular theodicean judgment of reality being better off without them. Theodicy involves accounting for the goodness of an all-powerful and all-knowing Divinity. If evil and injustice exist, why does the Divine not intervene? The proffered answers are that we as finite beings fail to see the greater good of this non-intervention on one hand and that the gift of free will makes us the ultimate source of evil on the other. In either formulation the problem is not with the deity but with human beings. This logic brought to societies has the same rationalization. If injustice and inequity are in a society, the ultimate fault is in those who suffer from it, not the society whose power mechanisms govern access.

This logic is hurled against the downtrodden in Euromodern societies. *They* are the problem, not the societies. What could one conclude but that the society would be better off without them? This means their present is haunted by the logic of their elimination. In effect, this means it is not only that they do not belong to the future but also that they *should not* belong there. Their present is thus retroactively delegitimated.

We stand here in the realm of double consciousness. It is where, as W. E. B. Du Bois and others observed, black people could only see ourselves through hostile eyes of those who reject us. I use the lowercase "b" in black here since it signifies diminished status. There is, however, another position to which to appeal. This initial double consciousness offers black people as a blight from which the society must sterilize itself. Black people, under this view, are problems. Our removal becomes, as J. Reid Miller points out in his aptly titled *Stain Removal* (2016), a stain to be removed. Achieving such, however, would produce the stain of removing the stain. Those long erased through butchery, nevertheless haunt the present in the ongoing denied memory of genocide. For those of us who accept the logic of our illegitimacy, the counsel is as Fanon stated in 1952: become white. For those of us who reject that path, our demand is for dialectical possibility. Looking at the system's contradictions, we seek alternatives. If racist societies produce problem people, why not build different societies? If elimination must occur, why not destroy factories of dehumanization?

An imaginative act of faith is required here. One must imagine belonging to the future, which would transform the present. But as that belonging would require becoming a being other than those depending upon their exclusion, the result would be a transformation from the affected black to the effective Black. This is nothing short of a commitment to Afro-modernity through which Euromodernity is pushed to the wayside as a particular modernity among other modernities. In short, the challenge for Black agents of history is white irrelevance. This does not mean the elimination of white people. It means realizing that white as White does not function the same as black as Black. Beneath the contemporary white is, after all, a white power structure that promises only one future without which there is the supposed "end of the world." Yet the question of Black belonging as agents of history means simply a commitment to life. As irrelevance and elimination are not identical, the point is that particularized whiteness requires whites learning to live among instead of over others. The logic of the system means black standing up as Black becomes a path from below to among.

Melancholia, then, is a socio-historical diagnosis but not a forestalled or ontological predicament. It is our condition but not our fate.

Etoke offers another conceptual tool to consider in the midst of this predicament. Her concept of "for/giving" addresses the tensions and failures of "forgiving." The latter is a concept saturated with bad faith since it is often demanded of those without power to bestow upon those with fantasies of guilt-free theft. It is the gift of deferred responsibility. There is, however, as with stains, a form of haunting through which such a gift is also a debt. Thus, it invites abuse since the owner of such a debt would ultimately like to be released from it. What, however, would that entail other than *not* being forgiven?

The slash in "for/giving" brings the tension to the fore through the grammatical openness of the preposition "for." By itself, the term becomes "for-." It beckons a relation that is open. "Giving," however, is also relational. It could be "for" or stand without a specific object in ethical openness.

Although Etoke offers this concept in contexts of harm, it struck me that its significance reaches beyond the corrective. What if for/giving were not the dreaded gift of forgiving but instead the act of letting go as a productive practice? I am thinking here of the complicated notion of political responsibility as acts of love. There is, on one hand, narcissistic love, which constrains others into the ongoing production and repetition of the self. That logic of similitude and sameness collapses into love of the self through which others are erased. There is, however, another kind of love premised on the freedom of others. The radicality of that freedom requires sufficient epistemic openness to the point of the anonymous without guarantee. In short, it is that open "for" in which there is neither for-itself (self-consciousness) nor in-itself (being a thing). It is selfless giving of a future to those who, freed, cannot be "us" despite being in relation to us across time.

This is ironic giving. It is gaining through letting go. The spiritual resonance of this idea, though well known in Western philosophy in the thought of Søren Kierkegaard and Simone Weil, extends back to African antiquity in the thought of Ptahhotep and Ani (among others). Rituals of having through giving remind us of the profound undercurrent of existence. Reality would have been perfectly fine without us. In true existential insight, then, for/

giving is also a reminder not to take ourselves too seriously. Achieving such, we may very well learn to live.

Not regarding ourselves as custodians of a gift for whites—forgiving— enables us to look at each other in acts of for/giving. Recall that Alicia Garza's tweet #BlackLivesMatter was, as she relates it, a love letter to those being bullied into believing they are not only unloved but also unlovable. This act of love could not be possible if one rejects Garza, a queer Black woman, as a source of value. In effect, her act of love requires the people to whom it is offered not forgetting themselves as sources of value. Valuing her love is an act of love through which for/giving is made manifest. In effect, it means becoming sources of value and thus transcending the immediate into those not yet born. What is that but also a transition from black (affected) to Black (affective and affecting)?

Etoke brings these insights to the fore in her poetic reflections on contemporary African struggles with genocide, Eurocentric epistemic claustrophobia, and global projects of white supremacy. She also interrogates these elements through unusual play on the feminine and the masculine. Nearly every instance of her use of the word "castration," for instance, is to a signifier or system instead of a male organ. Here I am reminded of her 2010 book, *L'écriture du corps féminin dans la littérature de l'Afrique francophone au sud du Sahara* (Writing the Female Body in Sub-Saharan Francophone Literature). That work is a brilliant study of the *corps féminin* ("feminine body"). The focus there is primarily the *woman's* body, which, as we know, is not always feminine. The complexity of articulating femininity onto woman is such that it occasions Etoke's insight on "writing." As a theoretical work, the question of writing here is occasioned by the question of agency, of feminine agency. Etoke offered a double move of irony and metatheory— reminiscent, interestingly enough, of Fanon's thought on his own writing— since that study, *L'écriture du corps féminin*, was the work of an African woman on African women writing, just as *Melancholia Africana* is a meditation on Africa and its diaspora from an African woman living through Africa and its diaspora. This question of self-reference as object of study and critique raises the question of paradoxes of the self. The self is, after all, always displaced the moment it turns to itself.

The observation of critical self-reference also emerges at those of performance. To perform the self is also an effort to produce what one is to become. Etoke rightly sees this through Black aesthetic production from the spirituals through to the blues and jazz.

Although there are many forms of Black music, spirituals and jazz articulate the poles of melancholia and for/giving of these mediations. The spirituals are born of the suffering of nonbelonging and the prayer of redemption. Demanding improvisation, jazz is quintessentially a musical performance of freedom. Improvisation is not, however, the narcissistic performance of the self at the price of others. In jazz performance, each musician seeks the best performance of the other. That is why the accompanying musicians drive the soloist for her best performance and in turn others receive such when it is their turn. They do not, however, improvise on the expectation of receiving such but instead on offering the possibility—of for/giving—through which there is room for others to for/give. Put differently, this performance of freedom raises questions of what may be possible if societies were premised not only on everyone doing their best but also on everyone being committed to providing the conditions for others to do their best. At the heart of jazz, then, is a political message that does not subordinate aesthetic life. The human world is, after all, a human-produced one, which makes art also one of its modus operandi of livability.

For this poetic theoretical contribution from Nathalie Etoke, then, we proverbially give thanks and encourage the reader to proceed.

—Lewis R. Gordon

Translator's Note

Bill Hamlett

Nathalie Etoke's *Melancholia Africana* is a text that revolves, dances, swings, and syncopates around an embrace. A call from body to body for a heart to heart, a lyrical cry that weaves philosophical harmonies through the aching semitones of a history that clashes with forgetting. I have been reflecting and continue to reflect on how best to articulate the specific challenges that this work presented for translation.

An interminable chain of decisions, any translation encounters technical and stylistic hesitations. Etoke's prose is powerful, striking, and clear. In a certain sense, her style mirrors her thought: poetic acuity married with conceptual rigor—an improbable couple. Yet, one language's mode of lyrical or conceptual expression cannot necessarily be resuscitated in another.

True to her poetic disposition, Etoke is fond of polysemic expressions. In one passage, she evokes how "the nudity of [her] being clothes her *maux/mots*." These last words are homophones in French: the first "pains," the second "words." As this association does not occur in English, we approximate with some loss: "wounds/words." In other places, such as in the key concept of the *cœur à corps*—literally "heart to body," homophonic in French with *cœur accord*, evoking the "harmony of hearts"—we chose to leave the French in text with an explicative note.

Furthermore, certain facts of language can distort conceptual expression: gendering pronouns not being the least troublesome. In French, it is possible to reflect about an existential human subject without specifying gender. Lacking this flexibility in English, we have chosen to employ feminine pronouns.

Other technical challenges could be enumerated with ease, but the difficulty that has weighed most heavily on my heart has been both pronominal and positional: who *I* am. For the translator, self-effacement is a supposed art. Yet, it is never innocuous, and especially not here. After all, I am male, American, and white.

In step with Etoke's thought, I believe that translation must respond to the complex social, economic, cultural, and historical situation of its becoming. This deep challenge was my constant companion, and resulted in a process that weighed heavily on collaboration. Etoke's assiduous involvement and input in the translation process has gone far beyond the norm. We spent many a Sunday afternoon on the phone, struggling through version after version in search of the most precise and forceful reconfiguration of her thought. As our process was anchored in conversation and exchange, she merits credit as her own translator to the translator.

Finally, in a conception of translation anchored in consciousness of the body, the highest ethic must be that of listening. It is a labor of passing thought and language through physicalities and subjectivities—their histories and affects—not an objective language science. From eye and ear, through brain, heart, and body, to the target tongue. The task was to listen (or read, as it were), *giving body* to these words in English. "Faithful" is a tricky word in translation theory, but thinking on this project has reminded me of the "leap of faith" that the leap between languages implies, like the leap through experience and history that language affords us.

In the ethic of generosity developed in Etoke's diasporic consciousness, "for/giving says *I* so that *you* embrace *us*. For/giving asks *you* to help *me* become *I*. For/giving confides in *you* that *I* may occasionally move away in order to better come closer." There is no more succinct manner to express what this translation act has meant to me. I hope that the ways in which the translation has moved away from the French have allowed it to come closer to the Anglophone reader. I hope that this translation will be received as an act of for/giving. An example of how those of us who descend and have profited from the pillagers may act with—by which I mean listen to and follow—those who can lead us into a broader humanity by facing our troubled past and present.

—Bill Hamlett

Author's Introduction

Nathalie Etoke

My silences did not protect me. Your silence will not protect you.
—Audre Lorde

I inhabit a sacred wound
I inhabit imaginary ancestors
I inhabit a dark desire
I inhabit a long silence
I inhabit an irremediable thirst
—Aimé Césaire

My final prayer:
O my body, make of me always a man who questions!
—Frantz Fanon

In a world where thought closes itself in language that strives to erase the sensitivity of existence, how can we make sense of sub-Saharan or Afrodiasporic life experience rooted in suffering born of social, economic, cultural, and historical structures dominated by unequal power relations? How can we examine the encounter with the Other? How can we understand a path toward freedom forged through pain inflicted on the body, pain that penetrated the soul? How can we describe a subjectivity in which self-destruction and reconstruction arise from traumatic experience?

People who were excluded from the universal family must face these questions. People whom the Other sequestered in the animal and primitive sphere. People who know that "non-recognition and ignorance can be a form of oppression, imprisoning someone in a false, distorted and reduced mode of being."[1] People who seem condemned to prove their humanity through time and space. People who have learned to live in the womb of death. Slave trade. Slavery. Colonization. Postcolonization. *Melancholia africana*[2] ...

"To be sensual," writes James Baldwin, "is to respect and rejoice in the force of life, of life itself, and to be present in all that one does."[3]

My process breaks with the habits that would have me speak of myself and mine as if I spoke of another, step out of myself for the sake of objectivity, regurgitate the Other's way of thinking in the Other's rhetoric that I have learnedly digested. In all frankness, I take the risk of injecting subjectivity into my words. The nudity of my being clothes my wounds/words with a longing to assuage, promises to keep, and smiles strung with disillusion. What I feel in my flesh and in my soul is life persevering. Life requires me to understand and to organize the real through ideas that materialize in everyday life. Everything that puts me to the test gives birth to an ethic of self that desires to speak humility, compassion, peace, love, generosity, and gratitude.

I will switch between the *I* and the *we* without any sort of process. The emotional, the genetic, and the historical interpenetrate.

I am not an unidentified or unidentifiable human, lost in the global village that the contemporary era aspires to be. My existence is anchored in a place, a history, a set of more or less haphazard, happy or unhappy circumstances that opened me to the world. The color of my skin, my name, and my country of origin are epidermal, onomastic, and geographic invariants. They help me situate my story in History. To grasp my presence without burdening myself with a complex of superiority or inferiority.

My freedom expresses itself through the flexibility, the fluidity, and the fragility of an *I* that moves in a universe rich with absences to inhabit, tears to let flow, fears to face, and joys to conquer.

An *I* whose travels across Africa, Europe, and America have fostered encounters both unannounced and overwhelming.

An *I* that reinvents itself endlessly to survive.

An *I* that destabilizes the limits established by monolithic History, fictive borders, the contingency and convictions that slaughter the Other, think of the Other as an object, raising walls of incomprehension, indifference, contempt, hate, and hostility.

I hope that the reader discovers herself in these beings constantly erased by color. A color that makes them invisible or untouchable: "Why not quite simply attempt to touch the other, to feel the other, to explain the other to myself?"[4]

By way of theoretical and lyrical surges, tied to literary texts, musical genres, or facts of language, I wish to unveil a misunderstood interiority. Negro spirituals, the blues, and jazz inspire the analysis. The Negro spirituals speak mental resistance and the permanence of a God on the side of the oppressed. The blues are a form of existentialism where personal irony resists the tragic. Jazz is the passion of syncopated or antiphonal polyrhythms where life crosses through fire without turning into ash. In the beginning, these three musical genres reveal an aesthetic sensitivity where endurance and tenacity lead to a surpassing of the self. To face the disaster is to overcome it. To submit to it is to die. My words will be blue notes.[5] They unfurl through conceptual improvisations, sensitive to the contaminations and counterpoints that tie Africa, Europe, and America together.

A writing subject, Black woman, and citizen of the third world, I refuse to be victimized or to victimize myself. I reject the position that would make the Other responsible for my becoming or at fault for my failures. This refusal does not deny the situation of sub-Saharans and people of African descent who continue to pay the price for the initial catastrophe. Like Walter Benjamin's "Angel of History," I only see "one single catastrophe which keeps piling wreckage and hurls it in front of [my] feet."[6]

Above all, I believe in the human being as a modality of the possible and of the act. The past, the present, and the future are examined from this profession of faith. The heuristic of pain affirms the inevitability of taking responsibility. What the slaves and the colonized endured is irreparable.

We have forgotten, however, that they did not merely suffer. Above all, they survived. What they accomplished to rise beyond their condition is sublime. If I am a professor in the United States today, it is not only because of the institution's recognition of my academic competencies. I reap the fruit of blood, of wails, of the dreams of those who gathered cotton over centuries.

The suffering of the sub-Saharan and people of African descent is not a novelty. For quite some time, a cumbersome companion constrains them to conquer the impossible. In this reflection, intended to be a preamble to transcendence, the relation to pain implies transformation of the self, action and freedom. Otherwise, the discretion and respect of the ancestors enjoin us to remain silent.

I am because we are. The alliance of the *I* and the *we* will reveal a complex interdependence. Thought emerges in an individual and collective journey where the *cœur à corps*[7] continually disturbs the established order.

What do I feel with respect to my body? With respect to the Other? The physical and psychological collision imparts a field of meaning where the fragility of the self and the Other manifest through harmful, voluntary, and involuntary forms of reciprocity. We must face the truth. No honest relationship is built upon deceptive foundations. I invite the reader to examine her being in the world as a historical entity.

"The black problem" cannot exist without "the white problem." Although racial division is fundamentally artificial, it is nonetheless an inevitable reality because of its anchorage in an unequal relation to power.

The past produced the present. Black or white, so what? We have developed a dependency on color.[8] We have inherited what the previous centuries bequeathed us. Either we revel in the figures imposed by an oppositional historicity, or we struggle to deconstruct them. Our conflicts reveal the extent to which we are bound. What brings us together is more terrifying than what separates us. How can we remove the mask of fear that stops us from creating a new language, from revealing us as we are, completely taken aback with this Other we would like to touch and who remains impenetrable?

Only for/giving[9] will do it. For/giving is a free act by which everyone gets rid of the inner weight that centuries of dysfunctional relationships created.

Hate, resentment, guilt, indifference, inferiority or superiority complexes, desire for revenge, alienating clear consciences, savior or victim complexes are states of mind to eliminate.

For/giving, as Martin Luther King Jr. highlights, "is not an occasional act; it is a permanent attitude."[10]

It is also a particular approach possible when the subject does violence to herself by putting herself in the Other's place. Thanks to this oh so difficult gesture, she gleans the moral consequences that impose themselves.

We must go beyond historical circumstances to prove that we are capable of creating a world to come where the past is meaningless unless we use it for the progress of humanity. The inner weight prevents us from accessing the most intimate part of the self, wherein lies that which requires me to recognize the human that stands before me. Whether we like it or not, avenging the original crime or refusing to recognize it is to perpetuate it.

In the following pages, the vehemence of certain remarks may be shocking. However, it is necessary if one believes that "to write [. . .] is [. . .] to disturb the peace."[11]

I oppose the apathetic decorum according to which it is forbidden to demand the impossible. I reject traditional zones of comfort and discomfort. Such a position puts me in danger. The risk has redemptive aims. Prisoners of a tragic misunderstanding, let us question our blind consciences. Let us allow our disarmed humanity to speak. Only it can reveal the truth of common experience. Every time I believed that this truth misled me, my fears collapsed and my chains were broken.

NOTES

1. Charles Taylor and Amy Gutmann, *Multiculturalism and "The Politics of Recognition,"* Princeton, NJ, Princeton University Press, 1992, p. 25.
2. The term *africana* is commonly used in the United States to designate studies, research, interpretation, and dissemination of knowledge about the global experience of sub-Saharans and people of African descent.
3. James Baldwin, *The Fire Next Time*, New York, Vintage International, 1993, p. 43.
4. Frantz Fanon, *Black Skin, White Masks*, translated from the French by Charles Lam Markmann, New York, Grove Press, 1967, p. 231.
5. The *blue note* is used in the blues and jazz to express melancholy and is said to originate from the African pentatonic musical system.

6. Walter Benjamin, *Œuvres III*, Paris, Gallimard, "folio essais," 2000, p. 434.

7. The concept *"cœur à corps,"* literally meaning "heart to body," is a homophonic with the expression *"cœur accord,"* literally "heart harmony"; the concept refers to harmony between the heart and the body.

8. It was used to establish the aberrant identities that are difficult to get rid of. Color is a *douleur* (pain) and a *doux leurre* (sweet illusion).

9. For/giving is what is obtained through giving.

10. Martin Luther King Jr., *The Words of Martin Luther King Jr.*, New York, Newmarket Press, 1987, p. 23.

11. Fred L. Standley and Louis H. Pratt, *Conversations with James Baldwin*, Jackson, University Press of Mississippi, 1989, p. 178.

I

Melancholia Africana: Scattered Fragments of Africa

A people that is unable to reflect on its position in the world is indeed oppressed.
—Édouard Glissant

So that though the European may feel that the problem of who he or she is can be a private problem, the African asks always not "who am I?" but "who are we?" and "my" problem is not just mine alone but "ours."
—Kwame Anthony Appiah

It's a bore just to be talking about pain per se unless something can come out of it that's constructive.
—Nina Simone

Chapter One

Loss, Mourning, and Survival in Africa and the Diaspora

In recent years, Black people in France—that is, visible minorities—have been trying to give substance to their demands by way of advocacy organizations. The Representative Council of Black Associations in France (CRAN) is the most famous among them. In the domain of literature[1] and scholarly research, a series of publications has attempted to understand the presence of Blacks in France as a distinctive group. *La Condition noire* by Pap Ndiaye offers a historical chronology of racial discourse in the French social space. Ndiaye carries out a theoretical realignment that permits a transition from "identity politics" to "minority politics." He suggests a form of "affirmative action" without targeting a specific community. In his words, it is "the wager of a balanced public policy [that] would both fight poverty in general and reduce the disparities between groups resulting from illegitimate treatment."[2] Ndiaye also discusses the dissensions among Blacks from Africa and from the Caribbean, separated by a "melanic and social hierarchy."

La Condition noire focuses on a minority that exists through the praxis of solidarity by default. This minority only has meaning insofar as it contrasts with structural racism that works toward the social, economic, and political exclusion of a group united by skin color.[3] Although the struggle against racial discrimination through the implementation of political measures is of undeniable importance, should the Blacks of France and of the entire world not also consider establishing a form of solidarity that does not take common socio-economic interests for its sole rationale? Any solidary action whose validity depends on a dyadic relationship with the French state or with whites must be problematized.

From the beginning, Black people and the African diaspora have existed through an externally defined identity, dictated by a three-dimensional process: erasure of initial identity, dispersion through slavery, then colonization and postcolonization. The subject is no longer Ashanti, Baluba, Bamileke, Fulani, or Yoruba. The Negative of the white, the Black is essentially apprehended through a paradigm of deficiency. When the militant and pan-Africanist diaspora adopts the *I* of a collective identity fabricated and imposed by the Other, the common denominators are race, historical tragedies endured because of this race, desiring an end to all forms of oppression, promoting a spirit of fraternity among populations of sub-Saharan origin, and contributing to the improvement of their living conditions in Africa and elsewhere. From a presumption that is both generous and flawed, we reconstitute a legitimate Black community.

Today, the totalitarianism of this initial conception of identity has been called into question. It allows the CRAN to fly the racial flag while demanding their rights. It also allows all those who refuse a petrifying globalization to rebel.

Author of the book *Je suis noir et je n'aime pas le manioc*,[4] Gaston Kelman exalts his attachment to the Burgundy region. Afro-Caribbeans affirm a creolized identity in which Africa is one element among others, in an infinite blending and intermingling. The youth of the *Tribu Ka* claim that they belong to *Kemet* in speeches that recall those of Louis Farrakhan, the controversial figurehead of the Nation of Islam.[5]

The election of Barack Obama to the American presidency also pulverized static discourses on Black identity. Although he identifies as Black, some in France still wonder whether he truly is. Others affirm that Obama is a global citizen. New epithets sprung up and confusion spread. A politically correct intelligentsia talked about a post-racial era, a "post-black" period, and a "color-blind society." The irony of Obama's victory is that it does not escape racialized readings. For many Blacks in Africa and in the diaspora, it symbolized a restoration of pride and dignity to those who were crushed by History and the opportunity to affirm their presence in the world positively. For certain whites, Obama's accession to the highest office exemplified reconciliation, a cathartic moment that purified a horrible past. For others, it allowed a message to emerge that would obliterate racial problems. Obama's success supposedly proved that racism no longer exists in America. It became the tree hiding the forest. Some African Americans have offered critiques of President Obama for not specifically addressing his community of origin. Arguing that because he lacks a fundamental constituent of Black American identity—namely an inseparable lineage to the experience of slavery—they do not relate to him. Barack Obama is consequently both the signifier and the signified of the racial question. The material and perceptible component, the color of his skin—because it is visible—generates an explicative logorrhea. This endless discursivity reveals a conflictual relationship with a rigid conception of the Black as an individual. It also underlines the obstinate desire of those who would like to absolve themselves of the encumbering and all-encompassing historical legacy that plagues the African American community and champion negative statistics: poverty, dropout rates, and criminality.

Paradoxically, all of these rhetorical contortions—"post-racial era," "post-black period," "color-blind society"—reveal the centrality of race in the relationship to the Other and to the self. It is too present, not present enough, or totally erased. Here, we can evoke the release of the film *Dumas* in 2010, directed by Safy Nebbou. Gérard Depardieu plays the mixed-race writer who introduces himself as a "Negro with frizzy hair" and "a slightly creole accent." Alexandre Dumas lived in an era when the privileges and disadvantages related to skin color were undeniable. He would have preferred that this detail were nothing more than a petty coincidence with no added value. Unfortunately, this was not the case. Evacuating that component of his existential substratum demonstrates both a memorial hoax and the excision of a past that continues to pose a problem. When the French of African ancestry were stirred by this choice of a white actor, the rabid defenders of the Republic cried out against communitarian degeneration and racialization of discourse.[6]

We read: "Dumas isn't Black, he's French." Does this mean that he belonged to a national heritage that could arrogate the right to eradicate a part of his identity in the name of the grandeur of his work? Does his accession to the Panthéon erase the *douleur* of his *couleur*?[7]

Couleur/douleur complicates the negotiation of a republican heritage that often omits its shadowed side. Why do some individuals demand a post-racial attitude?

In any case, it is always the same people who must rise above a difference they did not create by erasing how they are to become what they will never be. Everything happens in the gaze of the Other. Can we imagine white French historical figures played by Black actors who would hide behind the idea of a national heritage?

Sure. Why not?

Yet, if the Black can be played by the white, the reverse is hardly common. Depardieu's exceptional qualities and commercial potential were also advanced to justify his interpretation of Dumas. Does that mean that there is no Black or mixed-race actor in France capable of playing this role? From an ethical point of view, is it acceptable to amputate the story of a man and to invalidate a specific group for profit? Does the question of gain not mask the impossibility or the refusal to renew the collective imagination?

Racial demography couples with economic demography. Imagining a white Dumas is more comfortable when targeting a population that, one wrongly presumes, would have trouble identifying with a Black Dumas. Even if there were qualms, shouldn't we aim, through film, literature, and education, to defeat this predisposition that, far from being natural, results from a History that divided humanity in the name of color? The tragedy, after all, is the institutional and individual incapacity to accept the French of African ancestry who carry the stigmata of a terrifying past and the promise of a future. A double heritage, both disconcerting and rich, constantly stifled because it evokes a common past that no one wants to accept and that no one knows how to examine. A past that horrifies. *Dumas* could have shown France an image of itself that remains unknown to the public. This film caused tensions that reveal the absurdities of a society held prisoner by a theoretical anti-racialism that collapses before the history inherent to its establishment.

The slave trade, slavery, and colonization authorized human traffic and capitalist exploitation founded on racial hierarchy and domination. The relational and economic disparities between whites and Blacks in the Americas, Europe, and the Caribbean result from this initial power relationship. This is what inaugurated an abiding absurdity. Black and white are visible epidermal constants. We will live in a "deracialized world" when we all gouge out our eyes. In his book *Bad Faith and Antiblack Racism*, Lewis Gordon discusses Stevie Wonder's experience of racism from fellow students in the school for the blind he attended. Being blind does not prevent racism.[8] It is not a question of being "post-racial," but "post-racist."[9] In order to attain this objective, perhaps we should deconstruct the color that awakens the demons of a History that many would like to forget, while others reappropriate it, investing it with a political *telos*.

The massive identification with black skin does not account for the fissures and fractures within an African diaspora that problematizes and "strategizes" racial belonging according to geographical, ideological, historical, economic, and sociocultural positioning. The time when Blacks from Africa, the Caribbean, and the Americas met in Paris, Rome, or Accra to think about collective identity while elaborating tactics of resistance and liberation is over. It is no longer enough to worry about what is happening on the South Side of Chicago, in Haiti or Zimbabwe. Skin color and historical experiences no longer constitute the basis of a proactive and cohesive communal identity.

However, as racial hierarchization has legitimized and established long-term systems of expansion and exploitation, the becoming of a set of populations remains thwarted. The next generation needs to think about its relationship with the past, the present, and the future, dissecting the geopolitics that gave birth to "black people." The struggles, victories, and defeats of our predecessors are not all our own. The era we live in requires us to select what will help us move forward, to rid ourselves of what impedes us, and to understand that we do not exist in a stationary or victimizing relationship with History. Instead of enduring it, we must engage in changing it.

A set of oppressive circumstances castrated the destiny of the sub-Saharan and people of African descent. They doubtlessly gave birth to a Black condition. However, it is the right of the individual, understood as a modality of the possible, to invent freedom. Yet, this freedom cannot express itself fully except when under threat. Instead of understanding our condition under the principle of imprisonment, curse, or insurmountability, why not recognize with humility and honesty that it is the ground on which our future has been constructing itself for several centuries?

We have two options. Adopt a heroic attitude or become ensnared in the paradigm of victimhood ad nauseam. [10] After several centuries, the pointed finger of blame hardens into stone. Subjectivity finds itself frozen in an essentially passive approach to time and space. The victimization of the Black by the Other and by the Black self gives birth to stereotypical and dysfunctional relational modes that legitimize the Black's condition. To avoid this fundamentally nihilistic way of being in the world, it is essential to construct a proactive diasporic consciousness. Such a consciousness prevents us from locking the Black into the facticity of the Black's condition or in a temporal structure of the present. Because it operates exclusively in urgency, this structure can only manage occasional problems.

Diasporic consciousness articulates around a complex mobility between *idem-identity* and *ipse-identity*. [11] *Idem-identity* appears through a Black community united by skin color and the experience of oppression of which "the permanence in time constitutes the highest degree." Emphasizing "the different, in the sense of changing, variable," [12] *ipse-identity* disturbs the fixity of the *idem*. Ipseity reveals the desire that the individual has to exist for herself based on her lived experiences that highlight the need for a self-definition related to a permanent process of subjectification leading to "self-preservation." [13]

While keeping the distinction between the *idem* and the *ipse* in mind, diasporic consciousness functions in a tense dialogic manner marked by the acceptance of situations of precarious balance and disagreement, moments of disruption, conflict, and reconciliation anchored in truths that weaken certainties. Communal consciousness, however, eliminates the tension between the *ipse* and the *idem*. This erasure fosters discourses and behaviors that are essentially reactive and situational. Confronted with racism, discrimination, and exploitation, Blacks exist as a critical mass capable of changing the political landscape. This reactivity superficially unifies individuals of various origins. In the day-to-day, they do not really speak, nor take the time to get to know one another, and sometimes differentiate among themselves by establishing a hierarchy derived from the colonial or slave-system classifications. They also lean on their micro-community, which is itself subject to internal divisions and quarrels. One can, for example, identify as Caribbean, Senegalese, or Cameroonian. Then, for the sake of precision or distinction specify Martiniquan, Guadeloupean, Douala, Bamileke, Wolof, Soninke, Fulani, etc.

The Other's gaze obliterates the multiplicity of sub-Saharan or subjectivities of African descent by imposing racial characterization. To reject the totalizing specificities and internal amputations, we vindicate our respective identities while claiming a legitimate singularity. Curiously, instead of highlighting our intrinsic diversity, these identities reinforce sectarian antagonisms. Assertive identities imply a rejection of the Other. Disguised forms of self-hate or of a superiority complex, these identities are etched into a psyche that has internalized the racism that victimized it. They affirm themselves by resisting or devaluing that which brings us constantly back to ourselves. This negative alterity reinforces situations of suspicion, incomprehension, and conflict. The obsession or irreducibility of difference strangles a plurality that should be a catalyst for creating rich and complex relationships.

In the era of globalization, the idea of Black community is stricken with obsolescence.[14] It does not address parameters related to generation, social class, gender, sexuality, or the shattered geography that are inherent to it. A victim of the color that eradicates its heterogeneity, perhaps we should bury the idea of Black community to the melodies of funeral jazz, celebrating all it gave us. Would it not be judicious to abandon the concept of a community united by a color that annihilates plural subjectivity to adopt one of diasporic consciousness, whose authenticity would be uncertain, fragmented, disruptive, both painful and comforting? For an insightful consciousness of problematic truths that destabilizes the convictions of the oppressor and the victim, obliging them to accept themselves individually and mutually by understanding that what ties them together is the finished product of what separates them?

Consciousness that would examine the existence of the sub-Saharan populations dispersed over several continents considering the tensions inherent to their historical becoming. How to elaborate the gnoseological criteria that would allow contemporary Black subjects to understand their innermost feelings, evaluate the consequences of their actions, and the moral values associated with them? How can we develop a sub-Saharan and diasporic consciousness that would equip future generations with tools that afford them a better understanding of themselves and the Other? How can we reclaim the internalizing of a loss of self intimately connected to a range of possibilities that goes beyond the constraining and restrictive conditions that characterize its locus of enunciation? How can we analyze this ability to live with centuries-old traumatic experiences? How can we name the emotion identified by Fabien Eboussi Boulaga as "what alerts us [. . . to] what we are feeling, [this] self-affection made of suffering, heartache, fear, anger, but also joy and exaltation?"[15] *Melancholia africana*. . . . Let us examine and embrace this melancholy that colors the existence of Blacks in Africa, in Europe, in the Caribbean, and in North America.

An aesthetic of adversity and suffering confronted with a refusal of death, *melancholia africana* is an extensible concept that examines how sub-Saharans and people of African descent cope with loss, mourning, and survival in a practice of everyday life contaminated by the past. It is also the voice of a human being in her world, being in the world of the Other. This coexistence is characterized by disparities and conflicts inherited from the original encounter that interfere with the dynamics of social relations. Although it manifests differently according to the historical context and location, *melancholia africana* always evokes tribulations specific to populations whose existential promise was solidified by the encounter with the Other. Here, the slave trade, slavery, colonization, and postcolonization are objective, tangible, and implacable points of reference. Instead of paralyzing sub-Saharans and people of African descent in a permanent victimization, these references force them to act, to reinvent, to be reborn from their ashes. The world of the Other opens through the trial of destruction, of pain, and of weakness. Paradoxically, this negative triad creates an ethic of the self in which the absolute superiority of life rises from annihilation.

When we discuss melancholy in Africa and in the diaspora, it is essential to move beyond a feeling of profound sadness accompanied by a certain disgust with oneself and with existence. After all, it is not an incurable malaise in which the subject wallows or destroys herself. On the subject of mourning and melancholia, Sigmund Freud said that they express "a reaction to the loss of a loved person, or to the loss of some abstraction which has taken the place of one, such as one's country, liberty, an ideal, and so on."[16] Because it signals the ego's inability to mourn the lost object, according to the psychoanalyst, melancholy is a "pathologic condition" marked by "a profoundly painful dejection, cessation of interest in the outside world, loss of the capacity to love, [. . .] and a lowering of the self-regarding feelings to a degree that finds utterance in self-reproaches and self-reviling, and culminates in a delusional expectation of punishment."[17]

In Africa and the diaspora, a particular form of melancholy exists, rooted in the slave trade, slavery, colonization, and postcolonization. An affective state that is both individual and collective, public and private, this melancholy condemns sub-Saharans and people of African descent to develop a relationship with the world and with the self that is inexorably connected to loss: loss of land, of freedom, of language, of culture, of their gods, of self, of lineage, of origins, of the ideals born of the independences. Paradoxically, the multiplicity of loss becomes the terrain of survival. Contrarily to the Freudian approach, *melancholia africana* does not lead to mental suicide. It obliges the Black to resist decline, to revere life by struggling against everything that would aim to destroy it.

Beyond expropriating territory and inflicting pain on the body and soul, the violence that seals the encounter with the Other annihilates an age-old cycle of life. This violence calls into question a way of being in the world, exhausts beliefs, spiritualities, and convictions that until then gave sense to the destiny of the defeated. This intimate cataclysm also marks the beginning of a reinvention of the self. Sub-Saharans and people of African descent struggle to reconcile what has been destroyed with the newly introduced. The viability of the identity of the weak depends on their ability to negotiate the tensions inherent to their historical becoming.[18] By becoming, we mean "the changing of reality through freedom."[19]

The omnipresence of survival forges a particularly combative self-image, which corresponds with what Cornel West calls "black striving [which] resides primarily in movement and motion, resilience and resistance against the paralysis of madness and the stillness of death."[20] Owing to this constancy of effort against adversity, *melancholia africana* shows itself to be therapeutic rather than pathological. It is not self-destructive, but healing. According to Judith Butler, "in melancholia a loss is refused [. . .] the internalization of loss is part of the mechanism of its refusal. If the object can no longer exist in the external world, it will then exist internally, and that internalization will be a way to disavow the loss."[21]

In the African and diasporic contexts, the internalization of loss does not remain fixated on itself. It finds its coherence in an ability to reinvest itself in external space. The slaves, the colonized, and their descendants aim to go beyond the depressing conditions that the foundational violence engendered. The encounter with the Other placed sub-Saharan populations in limit situations—suffering, conflict, guilt, and death—related to the irreversibility of an existence at odds with the unfathomable.[22] Incapable of controlling, explaining, or escaping these situations, the subject must reconstitute herself from what was lost while integrating foreign referents into the culture of origin. Because this foundational violence creates by destroying and destroys by creating, it condemns its victims to negotiate an existence marked by a dynamic of productive tension. Destruction performed a profound alteration that ruined a particular structure of life. Constantly subjected to existential upheaval and precarious balancing acts, the relation with the self, with one's own, and the Other reflects the essential vulnerability of a collapsed humanity that reconstitutes itself at the site of its destruction.

Emblematic of *melancholia africana*, African American modes of musical expression explore the relationship of dependence between the internalization and the externalization of loss, death and survival, sadness and joy. In the spirituals, the blues, and jazz, we find distant African traces that survived the Middle Passage, traces interwoven with an appropriation and reinvention of European music, of Christian and secular traditions. From the beginning, these three genres—the spirituals, the blues, and jazz—have constituted a creative driving force thanks to which the sub-Saharan in the Americas attempts to negotiate, to understand, and to accept the Absurd. Through music, sub-Saharans affirm their presence and humanity in a new world that is not their own, a world that works toward their exclusion and reification. A world that they end up identifying with in contrasting terms. What was destroyed, what this people were robbed of, is preserved, as they struggle with external aggression in a reconstituted mental space. The slaves redefine their freedom by separating the reified body from a fundamentally rebellious soul. The limits of the chained person are not defined by her condition, but by her ontological potentiality. This potentiality may be defined through desire, will, and the power to create an internal domain where the subject in disagreement with her condition exercises her authority.

In contemporary Africa, *melancholia africana* manifests itself through survival tactics that test the limits of disappointment and disenchantment resulting from the failure of the postcolonial state. Because they were born of a complication of heroism and defeatism, hope and despair, dream and nightmare, these tactics neutralize becoming. The ability to act, to think for one's self, and the struggle against oppression are often reduced to the management of everyday distress.

An aesthetic of suffering confronted with a refusal to die, *melancholia africana* articulates a complex and fragile being in the world where everything becomes possible from nothing. Because it is born from annihilation, this survival displays an ability to be that subsists after the loss of points of reference essential to the individual's stability. The subject continues to exist in a weakened or marginal state. The subjectivity of the slave, of the colonized person, and their descendants expresses itself through the exploration of what keeps them alive in the womb of death.

NOTES

1. Published in 2008 at Plon, *Tels des astres éteints* by Léonora Miano explores the question of Black being in France focusing on communitarian discourse that personal experience continuously deconstructs. On this discussion, see Nathalie Etoke, "L'onomastique comme poétique de la (dé) construction identitaire dans *Tels astres éteints* by Léonora Miano," *International Journal of Francophone Studies*, vol. 12, no. 4, December 2009, p. 613–638.

2. Pap Ndiaye, *La condition noire. Essai sur une minorité française*, Paris, Calmann-Lévy, 2008, p. 297. Unless otherwise indicated, the translations are our own.

3. I do not include the cultural parameter nor the question of success in sports. The visibility of Black men and women in these domains truncates the debate by presenting a façade of multiculturalism as proof of a successful or failed integration. The 2010 World Cup and the controversies about the French team showed that players of Caribbean and African origin are French when they win. Their loss led to an outrageous confusion of poor athletic performance, Nicolas Anelka's inappropriate language, immigration, and the disrespect of republican values. On the television channel Europe 1 and in the *Journal du Dimanche*, Alain Finkielkraut affirmed that the national team was grappling with "an ethnic and religious divide." He said that it was "a team of thugs that only know one morality, the mafia," that "these people don't give a

damn about France," that they are "a scum generation" of "arrogant and unintelligent thugs." The philosopher passionately declared: "France is invited to examine itself in this mirror, an absolutely awful reflection. [. . .] France will contemplate the spectacle of its impending decay."

4. Gaston Kelman, *Je suis noir et je n'aime pas le manioc* ["I am Black and I don't like Cassava"], Paris, Max Milo, 2004.

5. Originally, this organization was called the Kémite Party. It became the *Tribu Ka* ("Ka Tribe," Ka for Atonian Kémite), before being dissolved in July 2006 by Jacques Chirac following a proposition by Nicolas Sarkozy, then Minister of the Interior. The members of *Tribu Ka* pursued their activities under the name GKS (Kémi Séba Generation), before dissolving that organization to create the MDI (Movement of the Damned by Imperialism) in 2008, of which Kémi Séba is the president. Séba also conceptualized the *mélanocratie* ("melanocracy"), an ideology of French Black radicalism. The High Court of Paris convicted him for anti-Semitic comments published on his website. During the *Tribu Ka* period, the youth belonging to this movement used the word "kémite" instead of "Black," which it contested as the creation of imperialist discourse that radicalizes identity negatively. Africa being a creation of the West, "Kemet" is preferable. Like "kémite," this term comes from the Ancient Egyptian *kem* which means "to be black." Kemet is Nubian Egypt. Identity is acquired through a specific geographic and temporal anchorage joined with a terminology that does not reduce the subject to the experience of slavery, the colony, or postcolony. For more details on the question, read the works of professor Cheikh Anta Diop, author of *Nations Nègres et culture*, a classic work of reference for Afrocentric theories.

6. As the white community is the most powerful from an economic, political, and cultural point of view, it is invisible. Its invisibility results from the fact that, for several centuries, the West has defined a system of thought and of reality that draws its legitimacy and its normativity from its ability to impose itself outside of its territory of origin.

7. In French, the rhyming pair *couleur* and *douleur* associate color and pain.

8. Lewis Gordon*, Bad Faith and Antiblack Racism*, Atlantic Highlands, NJ, Humanities Press, 1995.

9. During a speech at Georgetown University on October 10th, 2008, Michael Eric Dyson established this fundamental distinction.

10. Victim of slavery, colonization, racism, poverty, etc.

11. Etymologically, *idem* means "the same" and *ipse* refers to "oneself."

12. Paul Ricœur, *Soi-même comme un autre*, Paris, Éditions du Seuil, 1990, p. 12–13.

13. *Ibid.*, p. 148.

14. In 2008, George Lamming, the great existential writer from Barbados, expressing this thought during a conference at Brown University, affirmed that globalization began with the Middle Passage. Although constraint and oppression are characteristic of the slave trade, the displacement of goods and persons who were considered commodities is what gives it coherence. The dispersion of Blacks in North America, in the Caribbean, and in the Indian Ocean, the mix of languages, cultures, and origins, the abolition of borders (Western presence in Africa through its civilizing mission, trans-Atlantic trade, and colonization), the parceling of ontological and geographical space, all of this is at the heart of a widespread concept today. Although it was realized through violence, for slaves, the colonized, and their descendants, globalization is a reality lived through tears and laughter since time immemorial. It landed on them.

15. *Nourrir les esprits, entretien d'Achille Mbembe et Célestin Monga avec Fabien Eboussi Boulaga*. Initially published in the Cameroonian journal *Le Messager*, it was republished on the website of the review Africultures, www.africultures.com.

16. Sigmund Freud, "Mourning and Melancholia," in *The Standard Edition of the Complete Psychological Works of Sigmund Freud*, vol. XIV (1914–1916): On the History of the Psychoanalytic Movement, Papers on Metapsychology and Other Work, London, The Hogarth Press and the Institute of Psychoanalysis, 1962, p. 243.

17. *Ibid.*, p. 243–244.

18. The situation of Native Americans in this regard is cause for concern. The "discovery" of the Americas by Christopher Columbus destroyed the existence of those who lived there

before his arrival. Even today, Native Americans have not recovered from 1492. Will they ever? These peoples continue to live out a slow death at the margins of the "American dream."

19. Søren Kierkegaard, *Miettes philosophiques. Le Concept de l'angoisse. Traité du désespoir*, Paris, Gallimard, 1990, p. 118.

20. Cornel West, "Black Strivings in the Twilight of Civilization," *The Cornel West Reader*, New York, Basic Civitas Books, 2000, p. 103.

21. Judith Butler, "Psychic Inceptions," *The Psychic Life of Power*, Stanford, CA, Stanford University Press, 1997, p. 103.

22. According to Karl Jaspers, limit situations happen from the time where the course of existence is broken by something inexplicable and inescapable. They oblige us to become different people. What we originally were in such situations seems entirely inappropriate. The German philosopher affirms that we are confronted with two options: become more courageous or lost souls. *Tragedy Is Not Enough*, Boston, Beacon Press, 1952.

Chapter Two

For a Diasporic Consciousness

Through the constitution of a diasporic consciousness, I would like to introduce inventiveness into the relationship with History, the self, and the Other. I place my hope in an intimate knowledge of the scattered bits of Africa that only has meaning if it allows for the construction of a common memory that submits to historical and personal dissent. In the lines that follow, the terms *melancholia africana* and diasporic consciousness will be used interchangeably.

Diasporic consciousness is a sense of belonging that contributes to an existential fullness. It maintains memory by subjecting it to an archeology riddled with blues. The past fiddles with the present. The past reminds the present of its responsibilities. A present established on the ruins and stelae of what survived the destruction, and what was born of it.

Diasporic consciousness is flexible and open. It integrates pain as a catalyst of freedom and not as a factor of victimization. By ending fratricidal wars, it embraces the intrinsic diversity that defines it. It claims all those who constitute it, moving toward a cathartic encounter of Blacks from Africa, the Caribbean, and America. It puts for/giving at the heart of the relational dynamic between the self and others, in order to apprehend the "surplus of strange happiness" that reconciliation offers.[1] Diasporic consciousness develops an ethic of generosity. For/giving says *I* so that *you* embrace *us*. For/giving asks *you* to help *me* become *I*. For/giving confides in *you* that *I* may occasionally move away in order to better come closer.

If diasporic consciousness had to reconceptualize Pan-Africanism, it would be born the night when stars fell into Death. By hiding the plurality of identity under color, the hold of the slave ship unified this consciousness in the pain of a love confronted with the Absurd.

If diasporic consciousness were a language, it would be the language of the Other that became our own. The only language that consolidates the divided brother/sisterhood by anchoring the instinct of domination in a dissonant temperament. Tectonic, erotic, and corrosive, this language marinated in cassava, spices . . . found its way into cod fritters, boudin, gumbo, and cornbread. Creole, Ebonics, pidgin-English, patois, *petit-nègre* . . . language made of bric-a-brac, the bluish utopia of a destiny riddled with holes.

If diasporic consciousness were a musical genre, it would inevitably be jazz.[2] Dissonance. . . . The *cœur à corps*[3] of harmony and disharmony dissolving into one another. . . . Call and response. . . . The moments of tension when musicians rivaling in virtuosity attain a paroxysmal intensity, breathless in the (ir)regular lulls, elusive intervals where "giving and receiving meet."[4] Tormented mysticism rooted in the blues, work songs, and spirituals.[5] All of this music bound to weakness and suffering, to give strength, to sing the infinity of the possible, to free the rebel soul that flouts the reified body. A blend of a lacerated African heritage and the appropriation of European instruments, jazz reinvents a flexible identity out of a more or less solid one that was violated. This musical genre embraces the ambivalence of a thwarted destiny.

To exist freely, the contemporary Black person must accept herself as an aporetic *I* born from destruction brought on by the encounter with the Other. Destruction that immediately prompted a reconstruction, a reinvention of the self from what was annihilated. Resounding tears of a possible rebirth through agony, the cry and the moan transform into the music of the soul. Frightened, the Black gets drunk on the bitter water of resignation. Only this water grants the odd tranquility that can establish a singular balance between loss, mourning, and survival. This constant balancing act, subjected to terrible ordeals, reinforces the hope that germinated in the Absurd.[6] Desire hangs on to the barbed asperities of metallic life. It becomes a mental strength capable of blurring the borders of the impossible and the possible, nothingness and the infinite.

The jazz impulse speaks the perseverance of life. Music of "nameless nights,"[7] poetry of "moonless nights,"[8] jazz gives a beat to the poet's words. "There is no despair so great," writes Léon Gontran Damas, "that does not find its death at dawn's crossroads."[9] To the beats of ragtime, swing, or bebop, jazz gives birth to the sniggers that Césaire cherished. Armstrong's sadness clothes itself with laughter that devours tears. Jazz lets out the vital wail of the human who refuses to die.

Instead of calling some the torturers and others the victims, diasporic consciousness advocates for/giving, a promise of the future. For/giving is unrelated to forgetting.

For/giving did not die on Gorée Island.

For/giving did not die at Ouidah.

For/giving did not die in Elmina.

For/giving did not die on the trans-Atlantic crossing.

For/giving did not die in the fields of cotton, tobacco, or sugarcane. For/giving did not die under the lashes of whips. For/giving did not die with Emmett Till.[10]

For/giving did not die in a Birmingham church where the murder of four angels revealed to the United States and the world that evil does not fear the sacred.

For/giving did not die in the scarlet stripes of lynched suns. For/giving did not die at Sharpeville.[11]

For/giving did not die in Thiaroye.[12]

For/giving did not die in Katanga.

For/giving did not die. . . . Spattered with red, it steeps in a mix of sweat, urine, excrement, tears, and rebel laughter that mourns oblivion.

For/giving traces the *contours of the coming day*.

The ancestors were defeated. Before laying down arms, they often resisted. Many died in combat. Piled in the valley of the shadow of oblivion, their dry bones exhale life. Amassed in the blue cenotaph, the wandering souls of the underwater necropolis let out the rough groans of a voiceless heroism. In the face of defeat, there is often great courage.

Those who were defeated stood back up. They continue to march onward, carrying this great suffering that the Other refuses to see. Cumbersome companions, denial of responsibility and self-flagellation cloud vision. When will we understand that it is not a matter of guilt, nor redemptive masochism, nor victimization, but instead of a fragility shared in a divisive silence? Will the white and the Black ever be free without examining the History that tore apart their souls? When will they finally recognize the mutual vulnerability that the past cemented in *cœur à corps*? When will we confront this horrible anxiety, mirror of a desire for the Other? Will our History ever seize a dawn full of promise, rather than distress?

The Black's destiny was castrated. The white's as well. By constructing a relationship to difference anchored in hierarchization and subjugation, the white amputated his soul. Dehumanizing the Other is to dehumanize oneself. Draped in virtuous arrogance, the West continues to give lessons while refusing to take them from anyone else. When will it ask itself why it needed to create the *Nègre*?[13] Establish the slave trade and colonization to respond to its universalist and capitalist ambitions? What is one to make of this civilization that while proclaiming the sanctity of freedom, covers humanity in a color that rationalizes subjection in the name of profit and the accumulation of wealth? The day that we celebrate the History of some in counterpoint with the adversity it poured down onto others, maybe the dawn will finally show its promise.

Diasporic consciousness adheres to W. E. B. Du Bois's creed, which defined his attachment to Africa and to his people through an unspeakable feeling. This feeling, the irresistible need to nod your head, to tap your foot or clap your hands, takes over audiences listening to the choir singing gospel at the Abyssinian Baptist Church in Harlem. This feeling is the "tchip" in Africa and the Caribbean, but less common in the United States.[14] This feeling is a way of making the person you are talking to understand you are listening, agreeing with what they are saying by letting out humming sounds that others might find strange. This feeling is in the faces you pass by on the South Side of Chicago, faces that transport me to Douala or Strasbourg Saint-Denis. I get this feeling when I eat at Sylvia's, an African American restaurant in Harlem, New York City, where the warmth of aromas and the hospitality make me feel like I am with family. All while reminding me of the scents of my African childhood, *soulfood* invites me to new explorations of flavor. The laughs, the attitudes, the resonances, and the fragrances tell me that the separation was accidental.

Diasporic consciousness explores the "zone of non-being, an extraordinarily sterile and arid region, an utterly naked declivity where an authentic upheaval can be born."[15] It cares for its fragility, seals off its cracks, bandages its wounds. This repairing tenderness strengthens the self.

Diasporic consciousness does not satisfy itself with celebrating its heroes and its empires of old. Kemet. . . . The Black pharaohs. . . . Soundiata Keita. . . . The Queen Nzingha. . . . Harriet Tubman. . . . Olaudah Equiano. . . . Aline Sitoé. . . . Toussaint Louverture. . . . Songhai. . . . A torturous journey of the fist raised toward the open hand, diasporic consciousness is neither a pyramid nor a baobab. Kneeling before a scarlet abyss, it commemorates the wandering of those whom few remember. Diasporic consciousness lets out cries that oblivion swallows up. The motherland has dirty hands. "The dead are not dead!"[16] Ancestor worship! Burial rights! *Sankofa*! Oath of Bwa Kay Man![17] I am because we are! "Who will pay reparation on my soul?"[18] *Neg mawon* stand up!

Fractured memory impedes sincere homecomings. Fratricidal shame, overwhelming fear, languishing regret, and confused certainties silence us. Giving speech to silence, diasporic consciousness calls for a memorial unity expressed through tragedy, irony, for/giving, and survival. Molded in blue, mud, and blood red, diasporic consciousness allows us to live in peace with ourselves and with others. Instead of torturing us, our dead will finally help us live.

Shame buries truth under the dregs of the passage of time. Lies by omission abound in history books. Responsibility and culpability/complicity. Resentment and for/giving. Forgetting of memory and memory of forgetting. The unsaid betrays unadmitted tensions. We must stop confusing the author of the crime, the collaborator, and the victim.

How can we reconcile Enlightenment and darkness? The principles and actions that constantly betray Enlightenment?

"If equality among men is proclaimed in the name of intelligence and philosophy, it is also true that those concepts have been used to justify the extermination of men."[19] Ourika's distress pierces memory.[20]

Diasporic consciousness is wary of the universal, of humanism, and of the values of the Republic. For centuries, they denied its humanity. Riddled with bruises, these pretty words of which diasporic consciousness was not worthy caused the pain that it wished to heal. Pain consubstantial with its well-being. Diasporic consciousness would like that the Other be finally relieved of these pretty words. Why evoke the positive effects of colonization? Why ponder legislation that would have presented the domination and exploitation of humans by humans as an act that brought about something beneficial or desirable? To whom? Slavery and colonization. . . . The inbred relation created by destroying, destroys by creating. The match ended in a draw. Why spit on the dusty faces of those who hope that the foundational suffering of impossible love finally be recognized?

Without a lifebuoy, diasporic consciousness navigates the torrential waters of History, blending opposites. It tears the pages from the dictionary that still enounce in black and white the paradigm of an opposition without possibility of remittance. How to embrace a language in which I am constantly in danger? How to talk about a real and sincere evolution when language remains prisoner of a perverse semiotics? The noun/adjectives black and white are defined in the following manner:

Black, characterized by the absence of color. That has a dark color. Threat of failure, trouble, misfortune. Plunged in obscurity. That inspires anxiety, melancholy, that is terrifying. That manifests pessimism, sadness, adversity. Inspired by perversity, meanness, anger. That is reprehensible, immoral, or illegal. Very dirty, filthy. That belongs to a race characterized essentially by a very dark pigmentation of the skin. Synonyms: gloomy, preoccupied, African.

White, that combines all the colors on the solar spectrum, having the color of snow, of milk. That is of a light shade, shining by opposition with what, in the same species, could be dark. Man, woman of the white race. Synonyms: pure, blank, clean, immaculate, innocent. The hour has come to create an idiom that abandons division for union, destruction for construction. There is Black in the white and white in the Black.

Some people of African descent dissolve happily into a self-referential universe that solidifies a mutilated identity. They embrace the neoliberal values that engender a pathological individualism. Convinced they have transcended *couleur/douleur*, they are hard workers, educated, different, particularly gifted, thankful, and respectful of their home country. They do not identify with the handicapped population that continues to bear the cross of History. To succeed, you have to howl with the wolves. Adopt their dogma without blasphemy. Cover yourself with blue, white, red, cleaning up the *Nègre* blood with a pressure hose. Weigh down those who look like you with a congenital inability by advising them to forget. All this memory immobilizes. Mental self-flagellation born out of nothingness. Would it not be better to pretend like nothing happened? Drown in a perforated memory? Accept being blinded by the progress made? Cover your ears to avoid the speech of an age-old tragedy that urinates on illusory happiness?

The past will not die as long as the present reproduces structures of domination. We are both the products and the agents of History. Diasporic consciousness remembers, in the hope that justice be done. It invites the Other to cross the confines of this shattered existence. The Other refuses. Although the rejection is painful, diasporic consciousness will never transform into that strangled memory that expresses repressed sadness through rage and tenderness flayed by violence.

In rebellion against collective amnesia and disregard for identity, the person of African descent from *"sous-France"*[21] and from the *"lieubannie"*[22] is engulfed in a radical resurgence of awareness. She terrifies public opinion, the political class, and the caste of the politically correct. French people of African ancestry are forbidden to express a complex identity, inseparable from initial power relations. Because it apprehends the experience of slavery and colonization through a paradigm of repression, republican rhetoric created a psychosis of memory in those who see themselves as injured. Freedom. Equality. Fraternity. The motto is certainly color-blind, but History and citizens are not. When egalitarian principles seem inapplicable or incapable of reversing discriminatory attitudes, the French Blacks pulverize blue, white, red.[23]

Their Frenchness is a disillusion. Going back in time, they see that the values their country proclaims have not always been recognized. They belong to a series of unkept or broken promises. Covered in affliction, traumatic memories resurge. This pain is not silent. They respond with fury. Instead of slaughtering "the fool," maddened by his venomous speech, we must identify what in our society contributes to this sickness and get rid of it.[24] Contrary to appearances, the pathology is neither spontaneous nor marginal. The apple doesn't fall far from the tree. On account of the mental castration perpetuated by an environment that consolidates suffering, demands transform into drivel. Cries of distress and of love petrify. Stones thrown in the face of other victims externalize the torment of those who converse with a voiceless History. *Forfeiture of nationality! Love France or leave it!* As long as the presence of French people of African origin is exclusively considered through the lens of immigration, hospitality, and insecurity, they will never become part of the national imagination in an inclusive perspective. They will always be the enemy on the inside, constantly referred back to an eccentricity written on their faces. Rejection constitutes the fundamental trait of identity. It defines the relationship with the self and Other.

Unfulfilled, the desire for recognition becomes depressive. Having scraped so often against the arrogance of silence, shards of frustration make sparks that reduce the future to ashes. The antagonistic relationship between Black and Jewish communities results from an unfortunate misunderstanding anchored in a will for justice. The rivalry of memories is obscene and self-destructive. No matter the winner, in the end, Humanity loses. By affirming the specificity of the pain of some to the detriment of others', the competition of memories authorizes a racial hierarchization that pulverizes the pertinence of conversation. Whether one is of European Jewish or sub-Saharan origins, by comparing the Shoah and the slave trade in a perspective of differentiation or assimilation related to a desire for legitimacy or recognition,[25] we reproduce the aberrations that we are trying to denounce.[26] Diasporic consciousness reaches out to all those whom they wished to exterminate and to all those who refused to die. Pain has neither color nor border. It lives in the country of the soul. "Southern trees bear a strange fruit, blood on the leaves and blood at the root, black body swinging in the Southern breeze, strange fruit hanging from the poplar trees."[27] Lady Day sings to words of Abel Meeropol. Anne Frank reads her diary to Emmett Till.

Diasporic consciousness has learned that requiring excuses from the torturer is absolutely worthless. Is for/giving for the self or for the Other? If the Other believes that she has committed no fault, so be it. To forgive her is to forgive oneself, to free oneself from the power the Other exercises over our thoughts. Thoughts that condition our becoming. When it is reciprocal, for/giving liberates one from moral debt and repressed impulses that reduce the victim and the aggressor to an animal humanity. For/giving is not imposed. Without repairing the irreparable, it nonetheless provides a chance for common becoming. The one who asks for for/giving restitutes the other's respect, dignity, and integrity, that she lacerated through her actions and words. When it is sincere, for/giving displaces the present parties on a terrain of mutual vulnerability, the only space conducive to true reconciliation. The fragility of the wounded fuses with the fragility of the one who feels painful emotions—shame, sorrow, regret, guilt—born from the pain imposed on the Other. Mutual liberation and complex progression where an encounter is possible through voluntary action, for/giving does not obey constraints. One cannot beg for for/giving. Why do we tirelessly seek the rough embrace of those who endlessly spit on these clayey faces? Obligatory repentance establishes a new economy of the memorial divide.[28]

Melancholia africana, diasporic consciousness, African, Afropean, Afro-Caribbean, and African American. . . . Unconditional affirmation of an absurd, tragic, and ironic hope. Key to an existence riddled with holes that opens the door to tomorrow. A vision founded on tangible and eternal values that elevate humankind. Thick sadness of the night fading into the intoxicating joy of dawn. Supreme breath of love from a lyrical Coltrane. Bitter sugar that caramelizes internal scars where the dream germinated. You fight against the nihilism of pathetic destiny. Your children are swallowed up by death. They murder the promise. You whisper to the scattered suffering that tomorrow will come. Little nothings make miracles. The ancestors rebuilt their lives from a heavy emptiness. They built fortresses of perseverance and patience on the ruins of what survived. Edified possibilities on the stelae of pain. Humility on the tomb of humiliation. Slaves. Colonized. "Apartheided." Postcolonized. Are we what we wish to be? Will our History be carceral? Are we what we should be?

Nihil africana affirms that tomorrow does not exist.[29] *Melancholia africana*, you wept for centuries. You are still weeping. Weeping makes you strong. Tears from the past, the present, and the future nourish the seeds sown in mutilated space. Like a newborn babe, you look in the mirror at the blinding nudity of dislocated existence, nudity that invites tenderness, desire, for/giving, love, and life.

NOTES

1. I borrow this expression from Emmanuel Levinas in *Totalité et infinie essai sur l'extériorité*, Paris, Livre de Poche, 2010, p. 316.

2. For many artists and intellectuals of African descent, following Cornel West, Toni Morrison, Amiri Baraka, Duke Ellington, Miles Davis, John Coltrane, and many others, jazz is the metaphor for a Black existential aesthetic. John Murray argues that through a specific manipulation of sounds and rhythm, this musical genre liberates movements and emotions that can help transcend day-to-day reality.

3. See note 6.

4. I think particularly of the following jazz standards: "Koko" by Bird (Charlie Parker) and Diz (Dizzy Gillespie) and "Moanin'" by Charles Mingus.

5. James H. Cone remarks that the blues express the Black perspective on the incongruity of life. An attempt at a hermeneutic confronted with contradictory situations, the blues are fortitude in the face of a broken existence, the conviction that tomorrow will not be like today. "The Blues: A Secular Spiritual," *The Spirituals and the Blues*, New York, Orbis Books, 1992.

6. "Black and Blue," a jazz standard interpreted by Louis Armstrong, expresses the ideas of resignation and balancing through a melancholic melody regularly interrupted by playful intervals accompanied by lyrics that are both terrifying and comforting. Armstrong himself evokes the problem of guilt from the defeat of reason in the face of racism: "What did I do to be so black and blue?" He concludes his song by saying: "How will it end? Ain't got no friend. My only sin is my skin. . . . What did I do to be so black and blue?" Armstrong's song is a hymn to mutual recognition. The artist would like to move from negative alterity to positive alterity, to make sense of pointless cruelty. The original title of the song, "What Did I Do to Be So Black and Blue," was written by Thomas "Fats" Waller for *Hot Chocolates*, an African American musical played on Broadway in 1929. Originally, it was a lamentation of a woman with dark black skin whose lover left her for a mixed-race mistress. Armstrong's genius was to transform the message on romantic disappointment into a reflection on racism, thus evoking the emotional aspect that many continue to deny. Racism is also an intimate tragedy that manifests

in public spaces. As individuals, we invest the Other with a number of properties that make them untouchable, detestable, and liable to be exploited.

7. Léon Gontran Damas, "Il est des nuits (Pour Alejo Carpentier)," *Pigments-Névralgies*, Paris, Présence Africaine, 1972/2003/2005, p. 7.

8. *Ibid.*

9. *Ibid.*, p. 89.

10. Emmett Till was a young African American who was killed at the age of fourteen in 1955. He was accused of grabbing and whistling at a twenty-one-year-old white woman shopkeeper. In 2008, Till's accuser admitted to having falsely accused him. https://www.chicagotribune.com/news/nationworld/ct-emmett-till-accuser-false-testimony-20170128-story.html

11. On March 21st, 1960, nonviolent protesters against the Apartheid required pass law were massacred by the South African police in Sharpeville.

12. I am referring to the Thiaroye military camp where *tirailleurs*, infantrymen from the colonies who participated in the Second World War, were killed by the French Army on December 1st, 1944. Grouped in a transit camp waiting to return to their respective countries, the African soldiers dared to reclaim their remaining arrears at the legal rate of exchange. When the colonial authorities refused, they revolted and took the General Danian, a Frenchman, hostage. They freed him after they were promised their demand would be satisfied. Several hours later, the African soldiers were attacked during the night. Senegalese filmmaker Sembène Ousmane recounts this tragedy in his 1988 film *Camp de Thiaroye*.

13. In the American context—the n-word—*nègre* in French, is banished from discourse and public spaces. For those who speak French, despite its controversy and recurrent embroilment in more or less serious polemics, the word *nègre* remains a part of the vocabulary. Originally, it described a Black individual. However, because of pejorative connotations associated with this term, people generally prefer *noir*, which appears less marked. As a matter of fact, metaphorical expressions, such as "*travailler comme un* nègre" (to work like a *nègre*) refer to the slavery system in which work is simultaneously forced, unpaid, and exhausting. The term *nègre* is also used to describe the "ghost writer." From a historical point of view, the "nègre" is also the heir of a sub-humanity. The analytical effort here consists in bringing out the paradoxes and possibilities of a degraded humanity.

14. A linguistic practice originating from African languages, the tchip, or a "teeth sucking" sound in English, is a mark of annoyance, frustration, disapproval, or disdain in Afrodiasporic cultures.

15. Frantz Fanon, *Black Skin, White Masks*, p. 6.

16. Birago Diop, "Souffles," *Les Contes d'Amadou Koumba*, Paris, Présence Africaine, 1947.

17. A speech by the slaves who contributed to the organization of the revolt in Saint-Domingue (Haiti).

18. "Who'll Pay Reparation on My Soul?" A song by Gil Scott-Heron, available on his first 1970 album *Small Talk at 125th and Lenox*, produced by Bob Thiele for the Flying Dutchman label.

19. Frantz Fanon, *Black Skin, White Masks*, p. 29.

20. Ourika is the eponymous character of a novel by Claire de Duras. It tells the true story of a three-year-old Senegalese slave that the chevalier de Boufflers gave to his aunt, the maréchale de Beauvau. She raised Ourika as a daughter, giving her access to education and to the aristocracy. Despite her various talents and qualities, Ourika is "beautiful like the night." A character wonders: "Who would ever want to marry a Negresse?" Hearing these words, the narrator confides to the reader that she is "condemned to be alone, always alone."

21. Literally, "*sous-France*" means "sub-France," but is also a homonym of *souffrance*, meaning suffering.

22. "*Lieubannie*," or "banned place," is a play on the French *banlieue*, meaning suburb. I borrow this expression from the novelist Georges Yémy. He uses it in his novel *Suburban Blues*, Paris, Éditions Robert Laffont, 2005.

23. Pap Ndiaye remarks that "the notorious republican model is increasingly critiqued and criticizable because of its inability to act pragmatically against discriminatory practices, and even relativize them." *La condition noire*, p. 367.

24. I am thinking in particular about the words of Houria Bouteldja, the spokeswoman of the movement *indigènes pour la République*. Invited to a television interview, the representative of "descendants of slaves and deported Africans, sons and daughters of the colonized" declares: "We completely hide the rest of society and its privileges. . . . It is the rest of society that needs to be educated . . . the ones who we call 'the born-and-bred' because we have to give them a name, the whites in whom we need to instill the history of slavery, colonization. . . . The question of national identity needs to be shared by everyone . . . and that is where there is a lack of knowledge." Kémi Séba declares on RMC: "For five centuries in this country you walked all over the Blacks . . . we say this time is over. . . . We aren't here because we like the Eiffel Tower. We are here because a lot of us were deported here. . . . I don't like a country that hates me. . . . I'll leave this country when it does me justice, that's it. . . . There will be repatriations, but you won't have to put us in ships like five centuries ago."

25. In some Afrocentric American university communities, researchers reject the terms "triangular trade," "slave trade," "Middle Passage," and "slavery." They talk about the "Maafa," "the Black holocaust."

26. Motivated by the struggle for the memory of slavery and colonization, the Black French comedian Dieudonné affirms: "There is a uniqueness to Jewish suffering that makes it so we don't have the right to ask for anything. The Jewish descendants keep getting compensated for what happened during the Shoah. We, the Blacks, don't get anything because of some Jews who refuse that our suffering get put on the same level as theirs! . . . But I think the Jewish lobby hates Black people. . . . Since the Black, in the collective unconscious, carries suffering, the Jewish lobby can't stand it, because that's their business! . . . Now it's enough to lift your sleeve and show your number to get some recognition. . . . For me, my number is on my face! That's what they don't want to share with us." Because the comparison of pain and the establishment of equivalence occurs in a perspective of denunciation and non-recognition, the argument is both insidious and pernicious. Is Dieudonné talking about solidarity between victims, human suffering, or the relationship between suffering and power? Founded on an antagonistic tension, the premise of the reasoning contains the seeds of its own destruction.

27. The lyricist of this song about lynching is Jewish, the singer is African American.

28. It is worth remembering Nicolas Sarkozy's speech on the night of his presidential election: "I will return honor to the nation and national identity. I will give back the pride of being French to the French. I will put an end to repentance, which is a form of self-hatred and a competition between memories that feeds the hatred of others."

29. According to Cornel West, nihilism (criminality, ravages of drugs, problems related to education, etc.) observed in the Black American community is the result of despair and the lack of love experienced by the population that, in spite of historical progress, still faces serious problems with poverty, racism, and self-esteem. West does not subscribe to a conception of nihilism in which action and will fail because existence has no purpose. Neither is it a collapse of values. For this professor of philosophy, Black nihilism is a concrete and efficient response, a spontaneous and empirical reaction to the difficulty of daily life. Discourse on the self establishes a morality of "hustlin," an ethic of the illicit and of crime, that prospers in the groves of concrete distress. After taking on all the pain of their socioeconomic condition, young African Americans have developed a pragmatism of self-destruction. This paradoxical form of day-to-day survival is built on the porous foundations of immediate pleasure. Gangsta rap is the emblematic musical genre of *get rich or die trying*, a disposition of the mind that associates possession at all costs with the annihilation of self. In Africa, nihilism manifests especially through the semiotics of the everyday in which the incessant efforts of the sub-Saharan are confronted with the banality of death. It corrodes a destiny, imprisoned by pauperization, the absence of political will, and a lack of perspectives. Since the door to the future seems closed, existence becomes devalued. *Melancholia africana*, however, is a poetics of loss, mourning, and survival, constructed on the ruins of hope grappling with adversity.

Chapter Three

At the end of daybreak . . .
the strength to see tomorrow [1]

I encountered Aimé Césaire in my last year of high school. My neurons were not yet alert enough to understand the poet. *Notebook of a Return to the Native Land* [2] . . . an impossible enigma. . . . The words accumulated on the white page, the images, the metaphors; the descriptions were the source of my first literary upheaval. The more I read, the less I understood. My literature teacher tried to explain the work as well as he could to no avail. . . . And yet I had read Voltaire's *Candide*, Mongo Beti's *Cruel City*, Racine's *Britannicus*, *Black Boy* by Richard Wright, and other texts whose titles escape me. My unfamiliarity with the Caribbean, my immature brain, the naivety of my Cameroonian experience, exempt from racism as far as I could understand it, all of this impeded me from penetrating the work of this great man. This incapacity paralyzed me for a prosaic reason: "Let's hope *Notebook of a Return to the Native Land* isn't selected for the French exam on the baccalaureate." My wish was granted. Césaire never again.

Several years went by before I came across the poet again. As a student of modern letters at Charles de Gaulle University in Villeneuve d'Ascq, I dove into *Knight of the Lion* by Chrétien de Troyes, Du Bellay's *Regrets*, La Bruyère's *Characters*, *The Idiot* by Dostoevsky, Kafka's *Metamorphosis*, *The Blue Bird* by Maeterlinck, and other writings. Having made it to my master's, I found myself in torment over my identity. The years spent in France led me into a strangeness that I disregarded. To an Other that crossed my path without meeting me. Observing me without seeing me. Between us, centuries of violence. Stereotypes. Misunderstandings. Unresolved conflicts. Unshared suffering. Impossible loves. How to get rid of this deforming gaze? How to destroy this metallic veil? Reading Frantz Fanon's *Black Skin, White Masks*, I felt both strong and vulnerable. In this text, the psychiatrist from

Martinique mentions Aimé Césaire. I decided to return to the man whose impenetrability had left me with terrible aftereffects. Traumatized by *Notebook of a Return to the Native Land*, I discovered *Discourse on Colonialism*.[3]

A civilization that proves incapable of solving the problems it creates is a decadent civilization.
A civilization that chooses to close its eyes to its most crucial problems is a stricken civilization.
A civilization that uses its own principles for trickery and deceit is a dying civilization.
[. . .]
Europe is indefensible.[4]

The poet dares to put Europe on trial for its contradictions while claiming the ideals that it boasts.

And that is the great thing that I hold against pseudo-humanism: that for too long it has diminished the rights of man, that its concept of those rights has been – and still is – narrow and fragmentary, incomplete and biased and, all things considered, sordidly racist.[5]

He explains how dehumanization of the Other invariably leads to the dehumanization of the self:

. . . the colonizer, who in order to ease his conscience, gets into the habit of seeing the other man as an animal, accustoms himself to treating him like an animal, and tends objectively to transform himself into an animal.[6]

Césaire's cries never fall into hate or vengeance. Above all, they express a desire for freedom and mutual recognition. A thirst for belonging in a world that works toward his exclusion. Moving from the raised fist to the embrace, Negritude, writes Césaire, "results in an active and offensive mental attitude. . . . It is a jolt . . . of dignity. . . . It is a combat, which is to say a combat against inequality."[7] Insisting upon the specificity of Black experience does not lead to withdrawal or an arrogant Afrocentrism, which is merely a deformed mirror of the denounced Eurocentrism. By contrast, it is to recognize oneself in the pain of slaves and their descendants in order to combat all forms of domination. The encounter with the Other should not occur in terms of possession, servitude, or humiliation. Césaire proposes a relationship of exchange, of love, of peace, and of solidarity between peoples. The brevity of the *Discourse on Colonialism* reveals a dense thought that oscillates between poetic complaint, diatribe, and hymn to reconciliation. Rereading the *Notebook of a Return to the Native Land* provoked an unexpected reaction. Finally equipped with the lived experience that grants access to powerful texts, I got lost in this long prose poem that exhales anger to invite compassion, sheds tears to seize joy. Destabilized by my certainties, the suffering and punctuated words of *"ricanements nègres"*[8] forced me to explore terrifying spaces:

So much blood in my memory! In my memory are lagoons. They are covered with death's-heads. They are not covered with water lilies. In my memory are lagoons. No women's loincloths spread out on their shores.
My memory is encircled with blood. My memory has a belt of corpses!

. . .

Islands scars of waters
Islands evidence of wounds
Islands crumbs
Islands unformed

. . .

Oh death your mushy marsh!
Shipwrecks your hellish debris! I accept!

. . .

and the Negro every day more base, more cowardly, more sterile, less profound, more spilled out, more wily with himself, less immediate with himself,
I accept, I accept it all [9]

By opposing white and Black, guilt and responsibility, forgetting and forgiving, doubt and faith, could we ever come to a sincere dialogue? Starting from the wounds where contraries intertwine, *Notebook of a Return to the Native Land* allows an acceptance of the self and of the Other. The Césarian man affirms his humanity from his vulnerability, the irresistible need for the one who refuses to surrender to him. By revealing his weaknesses and his desires, he encourages understanding through an edifying and involuntary empathy.

> *Hear the white world*
> *horribly weary from its immense efforts*

> . . .

> *Hear its deceptive victories tout its defeats*
> *Hear the grandiose alibis of its pitiful stumbling*
> *Pity for our omniscient and naïve conquerors!*

> . . .

> *I surrender my abrupt words*
> *devour and encoil yourself*
> *and self-encoiling embrace me with a more ample shudder*

> *embrace me until the furious us,*

embrace, embrace us
but having also bitten us!
embrace, my purity mingles only with yours
so then embrace
like a field of even filaos
at dusk
our multicolored purities
and bind, bind me without remorse
bind me with your vast arms of luminous day
bind my black vibration to the very navel of the world bind, bind me, bitter
brotherhood[10]

. . .

NOTES

1. A modified version of this text was published in number 27 of the review *French Politics, Culture and Society*, p. 76–80.

2. Aimé Césaire, *Notebook of a Return to the Native Land*, translated and edited by Clayton Eshleman and Annette Smith, with introduction by André Breton, Middletown, CT, Wesleyan University Press, 2001.

3. Aimé Césaire, *Discourse on Colonialism*, translated by Joan Pinkham, new introduction by Robin D. G. Kelley, "A Poetics of Anticolonialism," New York, Monthly Review Press, 2000.

4. Aimé Césaire, *Discourse on Colonialism*, p. 31–32.

5. *Ibid.*, p. 37.

6. *Ibid.*, p. 41.

7. Aimé Césaire, "Discours sur la Négritude" in *Discours sur le colonialisme*, p. 84.

8. Literally, "negro sniggering."

9. Aimé Césaire, *Notebook of a Return to the Native Land*, p. 25–43.

10. *Ibid.*, p. 36–51.

Chapter Four

Pain that Sings the Happiness to Come

Nobody knows the trouble I've seen
Glory hallelujah!
—Spiritual

O, why was I born a man, of whom to make a brute! . . . I am left in
the hottest hell of unending slavery. . . . O God, deliver me!
Let me be free! Is there any God? Why am I a slave?
—Frederick Douglass

The history of black people in the United States is a history of struggle. Our
survival is a function of our ability to resist. We must struggle, we must
resist . . . to live on.
—Angela Davis

"They that walked in darkness sang songs in the olden days—Sorrow
Songs—for they were weary at heart,"[1] affirms W. E. B. Du Bois. Further
on, the African American thinker added that they "tell in word and music of
trouble and exile, of strife and hiding; they grope toward some unseen power
and sigh for rest in the End."[2] Commonly called *Negro spirituals*,[3] these
songs contain traces of African culture,[4] joined with an appropriation of the
Hebrew theodicy. A system of biblical interpretation through which a subjectivity thwarted by the collective condition affirms itself, the theology of
slaves works toward the deconstruction of this condition. The oppressed
flesh gives birth to an essentially redemptive prophetic speech. The enchained people identify with the chosen people. Like the Hebrews, they will
pass from captivity to freedom. Liberation is at the heart of a religious practice that justifies belief in a generous God, despite the suffering and injustice
endured in daily life.

The fundamental references of the spirituals are episodes of the Old Testament dealing with slavery, the book of Exodus, Christ's suffering, and the recurrence of death. Death's recurrence is a spiritual motif through which the inexhaustible imagination of the Promised Land and heaven unfurls. The intentionality of consciousness projects a sad event into an idyllic future. Assaulted in their emotivity, reified by their work, and constantly confronted with the nudity of an existence that they can neither disguise nor conceal, slaves redefine their relationship with time, with life, and with death. Deprived of all evolutive range, chronological time has an exclusively biological value. It testifies to the organic nature of a body submitted to the test of years gone by. The free person becomes a slave. The slave is born and dies a slave. The time of existence belongs to the realm of being subjected to and acting for others. Adversity and life without a future are its primary patterns.

As the privileged domain of the immutable, the plantation imprisons becoming. In this existential non-place, the enchained person endeavors to decipher the incomprehensibility of their castrated existence. Submitted to a set of external constraints, the oppressed person takes refuge in a spiritual space where faith in God and the promise of heaven subvert the situation. Death transforms into a step toward a final liberation. It no longer proclaims finitude, but infinitude. Founded on "this obstinacy [of the enchained person] to remain who he is, which is to say precisely something, something other than a victim,"[5] spirituals reflect the psychological tension born from the opposition of the reified body and the rebellious breath of life. They open a field of possibility where death is the precursor to the affirmation of life's absolute superiority.

By singing their suffering, the slave refuses to submit to an everyday life that denies their humanity. This suffering expresses itself through a structure of desire whose deepest aspiration responds to a sole expectation: freedom. The slave imagines this freedom in a spontaneous and conscious manner. Their captivity catalyzes an inner strength that is both painful and fortifying. Suffering battles suffering. For the slave, suffering is "the fact of being cornered into life and into being. In this sense, suffering is the impossibility of nothingness."[6]

The refusal of mental oppression constrains Black people to engage in what W. E. B. Du Bois calls "spiritual strivings."[7] The spiritual "Swing Low, Sweet Chariot" articulates this paradigm especially well. The soloist imagines her death in a liberating perspective. She talks about a chariot that will bring her home.[8] The "rhythmic cry of the slave"[9] blossoms through this story of death as the promise of a future. Death alone allows a reunion with separated loved ones and the beginning of a happy destiny. The soloist declares that it is "the brightest day that I can say, coming for to carry me home." Although the song is hypothetical, certain verses have an assertive dimension that espouses the characteristics of the prosopopoeia. As a deceased person by proxy, the soloist tells the story of her passing to the other side of life. The last verse, however, brings her back to the reality of her situation as a slave. A reality impeded by a faith that declares "the substance of things hoped for, the evidence of things not seen."[10]

> *Sometimes I'm up and sometimes I'm down*
> *Coming for to carry me home*
> *But still my soul feels heavenly bound*
> *Coming for to carry me home*

Spirituals explore the relationship between the conditions inherent to the locus of enunciation and spiritual resistance to oppression. The emotional flexibility of these songs, which convert anxiety into serenity and sadness into joy, expresses the paradox of a barbed-wire existence caught in the lasso of endurance. In spite of a liberating teleology, the plantation contaminates the matrix of desire. The spiritual "Poor Pilgrim of Sorrow" bears witness to this contagion. A "poor pilgrim of sorrow," the soloist affirms having been thrown into the world without the promise of a future. Life on earth being hellish, he decides to make "heaven his home." Howard Thurman assesses that the slave's lived experience profoundly influences his attitude toward death.[11] Does he wish to differentiate or reconcile his condition and his becoming?

According to Frederick Douglass, spirituals speak both to an immense joy and a deep sadness.[12] James H. Cone argues that they articulate a particular form of freedom.[13] Martin Luther King Jr. is convinced that all undeserved suffering is necessarily redemptive.[14] The titles of spirituals exemplify the productive tension that Douglass, Cone, and King seek to explain: "Soon Ah Will Be Done with the Trouble of the World," "My Lord What a Mourning,"[15] "Hold On," "I've Been Buked and I've Been Scorned," "I've Been in the Storm So Long," "Didn't My Lord Deliver Daniel?," "Lord I Can't Stay Away," "My Soul is Anchored in the Lord." The narration of a lived experience where contraries intermingle is at the core of all these songs. Waiting and acting. Fatigue and resilience. Lamentation and contentment. Doubt and certainty. Despair and hope. Sadness and joy. The oppressing present and the liberating future. Aporetic by essence, the lived experience of the slave modulates the irreconcilable opposition between her condition and her desire for freedom. While speaking directly to God, the human being trapped in torment develops an internal discipline. Whether sung in a group or individually, spirituals remain rooted in the intimate abyss. The soloist expresses distraught courage in the face of adversity and the Absurd.

"They can never do nothing to my soul," says a slave in the film *Sankofa*, by the Ethiopian filmmaker Haile Gerima.[16] In an interview on National Public Radio, Joe Carter, a spirituals singer, confided to a journalist that, during his childhood, he had met older people whose grandparents had been slaves. To the question, "How are you doing?" he said they would often respond, "All is well with my soul."[17] From the 1960s, the term *soul* was used to describe the culture born from people of African descent in America. In the era of Afrocentricity and Black Nationalism, this term occurs as a prefix in *soulfood, soul music, soul brothers, soul sisters*. Without necessarily being associated with a Christian or religious message, this omnipresence highlights the spiritual anchorage of a community united by a set of values and sentiments. "I dream of a land where my soul is from, I hear a hand stroke on a drum,"[18] the preliminary lyrics of the song "Afro-Blue" written by Oscar Brown Jr. reveal the centrality of a loss of self, consubstantial with African American identity. Related to the initial separation, this loss, simultaneously recognized, claimed, and denied, gives birth to a particular mental geography. The incontestability of physical separation espouses a work of spiritual rooting. The deported individual carries the absent land in herself. By taking a journey into herself, she explores an imaginary and emotional Africa that makes it possible to pick oneself back up.

According to Henrik Ibsen, the soul is murdered when the aptitude for happiness and for loving life is destroyed in the individual.[19] The effort of picking oneself back up as a slave bears witness to a resilient self-esteem. Spirituals are melodic "spiritual strivings." Although it wounded the souls of sub-Saharans in the Americas, their situation gave birth to musical forms that reveal the failure of a system of dehumanization, incapable of eradicating precisely what makes one human; this inner energy that confronts and overcomes the ordeal. Bound to an irreversible fragility from which she draws her resistance, the rhythmic cry of the slave is hope, endurance, and faith, all subjected to adversity. Spirituals formed the foundation of several musical genres—the blues, jazz, gospel, rhythm and blues, hip-hop—that negotiate the inevitable contradictions of an identity marked by foundational violence. An identity that works toward the liberation of a becoming, constantly threatened by the tragic history at the origin of its birth. Martin Luther King Jr. affirms that pain is a parameter inherent to the subjectivity of the Black American. It "emerges in the cheerlessness of his sorrow songs, in the melancholy of his blues and in the pathos of his sermons."[20] The ability to transform this pain into a liberating force reveals a poetic disposition that calls for and exalts life, thus questioning the depressive circumstances in which life unfolds.[21]

> *Through the darkness to grope*
> *With deep faith in the dawn*
> *And to manage to cope*
> *Until the night is gone*
> *Then to summon up hope*
> *And keep on keepin' on*
> *That's been the role*

That's been the role
That's been the role
Of the people. [22]

NOTES

1. W. E. B. Du Bois, *The Souls of Black Folk*, New York, Dover Publications, 1903/1994, p. 155.

2. *Ibid.*, p. 159.

3. Originally called *slave songs* or *sorrow songs*, from here on I will refer to them as spirituals.

4. From a formal perspective, call and response is one of the characteristic traits of spirituals (and African American music in general) that comes from the sub-Saharan oral tradition. It is also worth discussing the functionality of music in African cultures. It is tied to precise experiences: harvest celebrations, mourning, birth, weddings, funerals, games, religious and initiation rituals, ancestor worship, commemorating the history of the clan or the family. It is a part of the community's relational dynamic. Spirituals perpetuate this functional relationship to music in the context of slavery.

5. Alain Badiou, *L'Éthique: essai sur la conscience du mal*, Paris, Hatier, 1993, p. 13.

6. Emmanuel Levinas, *Le Temps et l'Autre*, Paris, Presses universitaires de France, 2004, p. 55.

7. W. E. B. Du Bois, *The Souls of Black Folk*, p. 1.

8. Some interpretations of this song imply that this term symbolizes the return to Africa, while others say that it could refer to the Underground Railroad, the name given to the secret network of volunteers who took care of runaway slaves. In the African American Christian tradition, people do not necessarily speak of "funerals," but of "home going." They celebrate the life of the deceased, rather than mourning their death. They rejoice in their loved one's meeting with the supreme Being. In this study, I choose to limit myself to the literal and religious analysis of spirituals.

9. W. E. B. Du Bois, *The Souls of Black Folk*, p. 156.

10. Hebrews 11:1.

11. Howard Thurman, *Deep River of Negro Spiritual Speaks of Life and Death*, New York, Orbis Books, 2006.

12. Frederick Douglass, *Narrative of the Life of Frederick Douglass, an American Slave, written by himself*, New York, Signet Classics, 2005.

13. James H. Cone, *The Spirituals and the Blues*, Maryknoll, NY, Orbis Books, 1972.

14. Martin Luther King Jr., *Where Do We Go From Here: Chaos or Community?*, Boston, Beacon Press, 2010.

15. This song also appears under the title "My Lord What a Morning."

16. Haile Gerima, *Sankofa*, DVD, Myphedud Films, Inc., 2006.

17. This expression recalls the hymn "It Is Well with My Soul," written by Horatio Spafford. The particularity of this response is that it highlights the effort of differentiation between tribulations and the state of the soul of the person going through them. Affirming the principle of life, the authentic "I" that resides in the soul helps the subject overcome the difficulties that she encounters. In other words, what happens to me does not define who I am. I certainly have problems, but my problems do not possess me.

18. Oscar Brown Jr., "Afro Blue," available on the album *Sin & Soul . . . and then Some*, Columbia, 1960. The first instrumental version was composed by the Afro-Cuban Latin jazz percussionist Mongo Santamaria in 1959. Brown wrote the lyrics.

19. Henrik Ibsen's play *Rosmersholm* offers a dramatization of soul murder. August Strindberg, "Soul Murder Apropos *Rosmersholm*," in *August Strindberg: Selected Essays*, Cambridge, Cambridge University Press, 2006, p. 64–72.

20. Martin Luther King Jr., *Where Do We Go from Here: Chaos or Community?*, New York, Evanston, and London, Harper & Row Publishers, 1967, p. 103.

21. This idea was also developed by Paget Henry in *Caliban's Reason: Introducing Afro-Caribbean Philosophy*, New York, Routledge, 2007.

22. Oscar Brown Jr., extract of the poem "People of Soul," *What It Is: Poems and Opinions of Oscar Brown Jr.*, Chicago, Oyster Knife Publishing, 2005, p. 77–78.

II

How Does One Make Sense of Postcolonial Nonsense?

The past carries with it a temporal index by which it is referred to redemption. There is a secret agreement between past generations and the present one.
—Walter Benjamin

And you, posterity! Lend a tear to our sadness and we will die satisfied.
—Louis Delgrès

Africans conceive the Absolute less as an individual than as a system of representations and norms bequeathed by the ancestors.
—Marcien Towa

Chapter Five

Scarlet Dawns of a Memory of Forgetting

I heard about the slave trade for the first time when I was nine years old. A student in fourth grade, I attentively listened to the teacher presenting the lesson in a rather peculiar manner. The history book and my classmates dressed me up in infamy. My ancestors had contributed to the tragedy. I belong to the Sawa people, a group of populations dispersed in the Wouri estuary. My parents were born in Duala, the coastal city open to the ocean, port of entry for explorers and missionaries, slavers and colonizers. Contrary to the handful of African countries where the traces of the Absurd remain visible,[1] in Cameroon, there is no vestige, no day of commemoration.[2] Nonetheless, colonization has its monuments, its hospitals, its boulevards, its squares, its streets, and its statues. Even the Wouri river, eyewitness of the age-old suffering, seems quiet. At the beginning of December, the traditional assembly of the Sawa people pays homage to the ancestors and the divinities that reside in the sacred waters. They ask for their protection. What must the unburied daughters and sons feel, who have been drowning for time immemorial in the torrents of a silent memory?

African thought grants a central position to the ancestors. Capable of acting for good or evil, they remain in the community in a spiritual manner. Many societies practice ancestor worship. The living bear a responsibility for the dead. The sociologist Jean-Marc Éla affirms that "many African cultures will never say that a person has died but rather that one has departed, one has left us, one is no longer, one has passed on."[3] "For the African," he says, "death is not the annihilation of a being. Strictly speaking, one is not afraid of death; but what one does fear is dying without leaving children behind. . . . Africans fear dying without leaving someone behind who will remember them"; they fear dying without "a community to which they will be attached."[4] Éla explains that the ancestors "can be approached with offerings and consulted in times of crisis."[5] If the dead are not properly buried, they become wandering souls who haunt the living, those who impeded their peaceful transition to the other side of life.

In *Scarlet Dawns*: *Sankofa Cry*,[6] the final volume of the African saga by Léonora Miano,[7] the suffering souls of the slave trade are at the heart of a contemporary story, which retraces the erratic paths of a series of characters who have survived some form of uprooting, abduction, abuse, or familial tragedy. The story takes place in Mboasu, an African country marked by postcolonial chaos: civil wars, poverty, mistreatment of missing children, who are kidnapped, forcibly enrolled in militias, or rejected by their families. In the Duala language, Mboasu means "at home, the space that belongs to us and where we belong." According to Manga Bekombo Priso, the term *mboa* "refers to the place of origin where a community of local people reside both socially and territorially; it is a group whose members, united by familial bonds, either real or fictive, occupy a certain territory." Priso highlights that the *mboa* is "the foundational social unity, from which the individual affirms their belonging to either a clan or to the Dwala people."[8] Because it acts as a cohesive social force, the *mboa*, when divided, thwarts the community's destiny. Miano reveals that the daughters and sons enclosed in the forgotten dungeons of the ocean give rise to the disorder that reigns in Mboasu. The narrative structure of *Scarlet Dawns* is characterized by an alternation between the voices of the wandering souls who denounce forgetting and the contemporary period marked by a becoming imprisoned by anomie.

With succinct passages framing the text as a whole, the "Exhalations" allocate a space of expression to parentage without burial. Rising up from the abyss, these "Exhalations" that reach the surface pollute the air we breathe. Living in the memory of forgetting, the breath of the anonymous dead speaks:

We are the bloodletting. . . . We were torn from the lands of our fathers, from the wombs of our mothers . . . [9]

We are still seeking, and now demand: give us the road . . . [10]

The unburied dead haunt the parturient. Invisible, imperceptible, they . . . penetrate bodies. Ravage life. [11]

They become the tumult, the madness, the chaos, the misery. . . . You whose conscience seeks to probe the intangible, here is the answer to your questions: we are the everyday absurd. We are the hatred of brothers, the hatred of self. We are the impossible, the shackles of the coming day. [12]

Let it be made clear to all that the past ignored confiscates the future. [13]

We are the rift, the chasm. Our absence is the heart of this continent. We are the banished memory, the mute shame. Those who have turned their backs on us for generations do not know that we are the air they breathe. We are the suffocation, the asphyxiation. . . . Our souls have become vengeful over the ages. [14]

Miano moves from forgotten memory to the memory of forgetting. The wandering souls do not focus on African responsibility in the nefarious trade, although it is recognized. [15] Essentially, they remember that they were abandoned by their descendants. The memory of forgetting conjures intimate stories and collective History. The characters are confronted with the troubles of their respective consciences. Although what has happened to them brings them together, the individuals' coping mechanisms for surviving the tragedy separate them, referring each character back to her own psyche. By privileging the experience of a set of populations, we refuse to recognize that it was individuals who went through a shared ordeal. We favor a massive absolute identification that leads to indifference. This denial of subjectivity erases the humanity of people of African descent and of Africans. They find themselves swallowed up in a process of passive essentialization. Frozen in time and space, they become what they were subjected to. The voice of the intimate abyss incarnated by the *exhalations* defuses the process of passive essentialization. It permits an "entry into the field of history . . . with . . . a triple attribution of memory: to the self, to loved ones, and to others." [16] In Miano's writing, this three-dimensional memory explodes. The relationship to the self, to loved ones, and to others is complicated by the consanguinity of the aggressor and the victim. It disrupts or destroys the affective relationship. Tacit forgetfulness then appears to be the only mental regulator of relational tension. While brushing aside the object of preoccupation or resentment, it helps Africans and people of African descent manage a precarious balance. Self-esteem is threatened by the reciprocity of a fragility inherent in a difficult past.

Miano short-circuits the oppositional mechanic that modulates the connection between memory and forgetting. The omnipresence of the "Exhalations" transgresses the dynamic of memory that would make of the survivors and their descendants the only inheritors of a duty of memory submitted to a society that refuses to conform to it. The novelist focuses specifically on the anonymous parentage remembered in the Americas and in the Caribbean, a parentage whose non-existence manifests in Africa by an active practice of collective forgetting. Through the "Exhalations" and her usage of the *Sankofa Cry*, Miano reappropriates this forgetting. She gives it an active voice. By deconstructing the term *Sankofa*, from the Akan language spoken in Ghana, we obtain "se wo were fi na wosankofa a yenkyi," which means "if you forget, it is not taboo to return to look for what belongs to you. You can always mend the fault." The symbol of this proverb is a bird that, though flying toward the future, turns its head to the past with an egg in its beak, representing posterity. The cries and tears of the *Sankofa* evoke a return to origins. This return reflects the demands of a memory of forgetting that torments existence. The injunction addressed to those who refuse to examine the past is posed from a locus of enunciation marked by the erasure of the event and of the dead. Forgetting as a complex phenomenon, both psychological and biological, normal and pathological (in this case, relative to amnesia), translates as a progressive or immediate, momentary or definitive loss of remembrance. It is also a more or less involuntary act that proceeds from a fault of memory.

Paradoxically, in *Scarlet Dawns*, forgetting has a memory. The wandering souls have kept and preserved it. They continuously restore it to the living. The unity of the self is manifested through the reproduction of a consciousness of the past unrecognized by the collectivity. The imprint of what was spreads through time on a continent closed within its History. Child soldiers, young adults in conflict with those close to them, blended families, the figure of the father and of the mother (absent or present), the loss of sisters or brothers, and intra-community violence are themes whose fictional coherence is situated in counterpoint with the memory of forgetting. "Every abduction of a child repeat[s]," writes Miano, "the separations of yesterday."[17] Further, she adds: "Us too, we were enchained."[18] The omnipresence of wandering souls locates futurity as "a form of being-for-death."[19] Memory of oblivion articulates the paradigm of consequences and repercussions that destroy life.

Again there was the noise of chains dragging on a wooden floor, giving rhythm to the cries of women and these broken words: San . . . Ko. . . . Ayané drove away her figments with a shrug of the shoulders.[20]

Centuries ago the course of things suspended the hearts of the mothers of the Continent in emptiness. Centuries, since the victims of slave raiding during the triangular trade, those who were never told they had a mother.[21]

Here: our furies are the madness of the day. They muzzle the weak, plunder the common people, consolidate the tyrants' power, crush the newborn in mortars, tear genitals to shreds, the women's wombs.[22]

Here: your days plunged in the endless night that we were given.[23]

Following the sorrowful saxophone of John Coltrane in "Alabama" or the weeping trumpet of Terence Blanchard in "Funeral Dirge,"[24] the "Exhalations" punctuate the narrative like a jazz funeral chorus. At regular intervals, they let out the rhythmic cry of the memory of forgetting. This cry slides discreetly into other parts of the story—"Laterites," "Blazes," "Floods"— situated in the contemporary period. Like strangled vocal cords, the "Exhalations" murmur a sad song so that joy can be reborn in the hearts of those who hear it, relieving those who wail. Miano aims to "articulate African history on the unreconciled, on disagreement that implies saying and describing in the African past/present its silent contour [to] restitute the absent chains that express themselves (without being heard) not in saying but in the half-said of the not-yet."[25] To carry out this perilous enterprise, the novelist uses the motif of call and response, which originates from an African oral tradition in which speech is circular. The one who speaks does not content herself with expressing her opinion. She does not possess the truth. Rather, she calls out to those who listen. Her words have no value unless the audience responds or attributes authority to what she says.

The call let out by the memory of oblivion finds itself confronted with an oral tradition that eradicates its experience. The words of those whom society has not properly buried or commemorated are spoken out of a discursive emptiness. Invisible presences who refuse to die, the wandering souls inscribe themselves in the temporality of the living. This use of prosopopoeia invites us to reflect on postcolonial being and time. *Scarlet Dawns* combine synchrony and diachrony. The correspondence between facts and events considered simultaneous challenge chronological evolution. The historicity of the individual and the periodicity of history—the slave trade, colonization, and the postcolony—are simultaneously attached and disjointed. The temporal dimension of existence has no value unless the human acts. Although centuries have gone by, human agency today mirrors the agency that prevailed at the time of the initial catastrophe: the "present is not passage, but the stop and blockage of time."[26] Miano obliges the reader to examine an oral memory that preceded the eradication of a shameful episode. How can contemporary Africa respond to a muffled call that it hears but is unable to decode?

What obscure thing gnawed the souls of the inhabitants in the heart of the Continent? What was the name of the Beast, where did it come from?[27]

An impression of suspended time. . . . There, I heard someone call out to me. Not recognizing the voice, I did not respond. . . . That is when I saw him. Eyia was there, sitting in the middle of a group of faceless people. . . . I could only see the chains that tied the ones to the others.[28]

The motif of call and response occurs through different modulations of the relationship between the self and others. In the preceding citations, the reader finds Ayané and Epa, two characters that had already appeared in *Dark Heart of the Night*,[29] the first volume of Miano's African saga. Ayané has finally returned to Mboasu to try to understand a truth that she feared. The adolescent deserted the militia of the Forces of Change. One of her brothers was sacrificed. She aims to find and to bring the nine others who disappeared back to the village. Historical/calendar time marked by precise events contrasts with narrative time fixed in analepsis. Constantly confronted with the need to dig up the past narrative—the present must be purified—the contemporary period is marked by tension. Because of the violence at its foundation, it unifies opposing poles and produces situations of precarious balance. The survival or the loss of the subject depends on her ability to cope with this tension in an edifying or destructive manner.

In *Scarlet Dawns*, this tension is deployed in themes of violence, Françafrique,[30] and failure of the postcolonial state. The fictive representation of war, hate, despair, and division finds coherence in the constant call for peace, love, hope, and reconciliation that it parallels. The narrative opacity reveals the depth of a trauma of the unspoken that enchains the collective psyche. The forgetting of wandering souls is expressed through several dysfunctional modalities. Visible to the naked eye because of the pornographic gaze, power relations and political issues in the postcolony end up blinding us. One forgets that "it is derisory and cruel to revel in discourse on democracy, human rights, in a culture of death devalued by superfluous and encumbering men."[31] Could the slave trade be at the origin of this culture of devalued death? The obsessional focus on the flagrant effect of the postcolonial failure should not replace thought on African being in the world. Is the thought process that produces violence and social disorganization not the reflection of an inability to revisit what is repressed?

Through the character Epupa, the madwoman, Miano thinks through this thought process by problematizing sorcery, rituals, and African traditions.[32] In Africa, mental illness is not always recognized. Psychological disorders are often attributed to mystical attacks or witchcraft. Miano combines the two approaches, as they both bear witness to a common etiological identity: the sickness of the soul, the mind, the mental faculties.[33] The novelist wonders: "How our culture has . . . come to the point of giving sickness the sense of deviation, and to the sick a status that excluded him [from society]? And how, despite this, our society expresses itself . . . in these morbid forms in which it refuses to recognize itself?"[34] The motif of madness is the megaphone of the memory of forgetting. Exiled in a psychiatric hospital, Epupa has interiorized the surrounding tumult and the voices banished from the History that give rhythm to daily life. Her delirious speech is that of a seer. She predicts the future, discovers and reveals what people hide, are unaware of, or refuse to see. Epupa allows for a return to a conflictual past in order to unlock the future. Because we live in the permanence of those and that which we claim to forget, the Pythia establishes the echo of ancient times in the inanity of the present: "Those who send me are from a time you did not know,"[35] she confides to a character. Miano draws out an approach to postcolonial malaise anchored in a spiritual relationship with the past.

The continental pain was spiritual. Tragedy unfolded ceaselessly on those grounds, engendering the repercussions that we felt in the manifested world. The fault did not uniquely lie in the trade of human beings. . . . The continental sin was in forgetting.[36]

. . .

If the dead did not disappear, as we believed here, if they continued to exercise an influence on the daily lives of the living, we knew, in our hearts, that in covering them with indignity, we condemned ourselves. . . . The time had come to stop suffering.[37]

Spirituality also accompanies the theme of childhood suffering. It reveals a desire to pass from the futurity of being in death to the futurity of being in life. The ceremony of reintegration reconnects abducted children and those who were driven out of an ancestral heritage of which they were dispossessed. The seer Epupa is pregnant. "The child to be born," writes Miano, "knew how heavy he was to carry."[38]

The theme of maternity is inscribed in an "articulation of natality" that enjoins us to "always remember that humans, although they must die, are not born to die, but to create."[39] Progeny is the essential message sent to a future we may never see. It introduces newness into what has an established character while living in the time to come. The children's reintegration into their original environment reconciles them with their destiny. A promise of tomorrows that will come without us, these descendants affirm the continuity of life, of hope.

Pain brings the dispersed parts of Africa together, separated parts of family, parts of wounded love, parts of a mutilated self, parts of the Other in us that we try to cut out, parts of *I am because we are* that steep into the crater of forgetting, pain, and silence. All of these parts patch together, mend in an ethic of for/giving. This ethic prospers in spheres of suffering and reconciliation that invite us to act and not withdraw. This ethic reclaims constructive ancestral beliefs. It purifies the past of its destructive substrate. We forgive the Other while forgiving ourselves for having failed:

It was asked of Epa to repent for his fault. He did so. . . . The acceptance of the clan . . . helped him heal his wounds, but distance was necessary.[40]

—Mother, I ask for your forgiveness. . . . As well, I ask for your forgiveness. It was not your fault, if your parents did not raise you according to our traditions.[41]

The structure of *Scarlet Dawns* draws upon the theory of the four elements that constitute the world. *Laterite* for earth, *Blazes* for fire, *Floods* for water, *Exhalations* for air. Beyond this cosmological imagery, Miano maximizes the symbolism of darkness, light, and redness:

When [Epupa] submerged her head in water, a scarlet sun had risen. . . . Silhouettes, that she saw from behind, formed a circle . . . they did not come to speak to her, clapping their hands continuously while one of them, at the center of the circle, traced several dance steps before stepping aside.[42]

The novel ends with a poetics of redemption when the sun finally rises: "The sun had deserted its hemogloblin red to gorge itself on yellow . . . [there] has never been a night, long as it may be, that did not give birth to light."[43] Red is the color of Epupa's clothes. The being between two worlds who creates harmony between the dead and the living, the past and the present. This red is blood. The liquid that travels throughout the body to maintain life. Blood is death. Floods of pain shed on the hard earth. Sap of our existence, all this red is the memory of those who refused to die. . . . At the heart of their suffering is the promise of our freedom.

NOTES

1. Gorée Island in Senegal, Cape Coast Castle and Elmina Castle in Ghana, Ouidah in Benin.

2. Since the publication of the book in French, the site of Bimbia was officially recognized by the Cameroonian state as a site of memory of the slave trade.

3. Jean-Marc Éla, *My Faith as an African*, Nairobi, Action Publishers, 2001, p. 16.

4. *Ibid.*

5. *Ibid.*, p. 15.

6. Léonora Miano, *Les Aubes écarlates: Sankofa cry*, Paris, Plon, 2009.

7. I use this term because it places emphasis on the centrality of family in the fictional project. *L'intéreur de la nuit*, *Contours du jour qui vient*, and *Les Aubes écarlates* tell the story of an African nuclear family over several generations in different spaces. These three novels include more or less historical facts transformed by the author's imagination.

8. Manga Bekombo Pris, "Conflit d'autorité au sein de la société familiale chez les Dwala du Sud-Cameroun," *Cahier d'études africaines*, vol. 4, 1963, p. 317.

9. Léonora Miano, *Les Aubes écarlates*, p. 11.

10. *Ibid.*, p. 13.

11. *Ibid.*

12. *Ibid.*

13. *Ibid.*, p. 14.

14. *Ibid.*, p. 38.

15. In 1999, Mathieu Kérékou, president of the Republic of Benin, organized a conference so that descendants of slaves and those of African people implicated in the slave trade could discuss paths to reconciliation. In 2002, Cyrille Oguin, ambassador of Benin to the United States, publicly recognized the participation of his country in the trans-Atlantic slave trade.

16. Paul Ricœur, *La Mémoire, l'Histoire, l'Oublie*, Paris, Éditions du Seuil, 2000, p. 163.

17. Léonora Miano, *Les Aubes écarlates*, p. 267.

18. *Ibid.*, p. 75.

19. Paul Ricœur, *La Mémoire, l'Histoire, l'Oublie*, p. 457.

20. Léonora Miano, *Les Aubes écarlates*, p. 24–25.

21. *Ibid.*, p. 35.

22. *Ibid.*, p. 38.

23. *Ibid.*

24. "Alabama" is a song composed by John Coltrane in memory of four Black girls from eleven to fourteen years old who were killed by a bomb detonated in a Baptist church in Birmingham in 1963. It is on his album *Live at Birdland*, Impulse, 1964. "Funeral Dirge" by Terence Blanchard is on his album *A Tale of God's Will, A Requiem for Katrina*, Blue Note Records, 2007. Inspired by the tradition of funeral jazz, this artist from New Orleans pays tribute to the city and its residents submerged by water in 2005.

25. Jean-Godefroy Bidima, *La Philosophie négro-africaine*, Paris, PUF, 1995, p. 83.

26. Walter Benjamin, *Œuvres* III, p. 440.

27. Léonora Miano, *Les Aubes écarlates*, p. 18.

28. *Ibid.*, p. 68.

29. Léonora Miano, *L'intérieur de la nuit*, Paris, Plon, 2005.

30. In a book called *La Françafrique: The Longest Scandal of the Republic*, published by Stock in 1998, François-Xavier Verschave reveals and examines the different networks of military, economic, and political influence that allowed France to exploit the riches of the former colonies by maintaining close relations with African leaders whose governmental practices were reprehensible.

31. Fabien Eboussi Boulaga, *Nourrir les esprits.*

32. These traditions include positive and negative elements related to an interpretation of the oral tradition that each person adapts for better or for worse. They have the ability to harm or heal. The father Eric de Rosny Dibounje, author of the book *Les Yeux de ma chèvre*, distinguishes sorcerers and anti-sorcerers, called *nganga*, in the vocabulary of African/Douala mysticism. Both have access to a supernatural world; however, they use their power differently, thus reproducing the combat between good and evil.

33. From an etymological point of view: *esprit*, here translated "mind," comes from the Latin *spiritus*, principle of life, soul. Soul, or *âme* in French, from the Latin *anima*, the spiritual principle of the human being. "Mental," from the Old French *mentele*, is what happens in the mind.

34. Michel Foucault, *Maladie mentale et psychologie*, Paris, Presses Universitaires de France, 1997, p. 75.

35. Léonora Miano, *L'intérieur de la nuit*, p. 235.

36. Léonora Miano, *L'intérieur de la nuit*, p. 198.

37. *Ibid.*, p. 266–267.

38. *Ibid.*, p. 259.

39. Hannah Arendt, *La Condition de l'homme moderne*, Paris, Calmann-Lévy, 1961, p. 276–277.

40. Léonora Miano, *L'intérieur de la nuit*, p. 248.

41. *Ibid.*, p. 253.

42. *Ibid.*, p. 267.

43. *Ibid.*, p. 267–268.

Chapter Six

From Death to Life in the Country of a Thousand Hills

Why me? Why us? Why here and now? How to be responsible without being guilty, without being individually guilty for the boundless consequences of what we do and what we do not do? How to impute to someone or some group what belongs to the realm of the superhuman?
—Fabien Eboussi Boulaga

May we always hear the mute cry of those who could not cry out because they were killed, those for whom only the earth can still cry out. May we be saved from despair in the face of so much suffering and misery. . . . May they live on within us, the men and their history that encourage us to defeat hate in this world.
—Michael Schweitzer

In 1994, the systematic extermination of man by man took hold in the country of a thousand hills. Literary works that thematize the Rwandan genocide negotiate the beginning of a new era without erasing the pain of past events. This negotiation operates through a narrative grammar of loss anchored in survival. Synonymous with a precariousness that is consubstantial with Africans, survival appears regularly in the Western media where Africa is presented as existing exclusively through the pornography of violence and poverty.[1] Only the obligatory discourses on misery, AIDS, and the atrocities of war are worthy of interest. This discursive paradigm overlooks the fact that survival has metaphysical implications that emphasize transcending the self. To survive is to resist the conditions of a sinister, tragic, and catastrophic existence. To survive is to refuse to give in. It is to say "yes" to life when it pushes you to say "no." It is to remain standing and raise your eyes to the sky while an uncontrollable force pulls you down toward the meanders of despair. It is to keep your feet on the ground and your head in the clouds. It is to rebel against anything that plots to imprison you in the depths of darkness. To survive is somehow to go beyond death without entering eternity. To survive is to transform the adversity of the present time into a promise of the future.

Murambi, le livre des ossements by Boubacar Boris Diop[2] and *Le Passé devant soi* by Gilbert Gatore[3] are literary works in which the theme of death highlights desire for life. These authors problematize the possibility of an existential fullness that surpasses tragedy. Here, death is related to an idea of life with death, of life after death, and life beyond death. As fictive explorations of a real human disaster, the works by Diop and Gatore show how personal history is confronted with national history and vice versa. By focusing on specific characters, the novel deconstructs the totalitarian anonymity of the media report, which confines populations into descriptions where horror and cruelty become aberrant identity markers. The narrative experience focuses on the process of negotiation and tension, harmony and dissonance, constitutive of a subjectivity struggling against loss, grief, and survival.

Murambi, le livre des ossements tells the story of Cornelius Uvimana's return to Rwanda, four years after the genocide. Exiled in Djibouti at the time of the turmoil, this Rwandan with a Hutu father and a Tutsi mother returns to his native country to inquire about his loved ones. His father, the doctor Joseph Karekezi, actively participated in the Murambi massacres that took the lives of his mother, brothers, and sisters. In Diop's novel, survival manifests through a complicated negotiation of the past and the present:

In disparate fragments, scenes from the past and the present cross in his memory. He felt how difficult it would be to put his life in order. . . . To return to his country—to be happy or to suffer there—was a rebirth.[4]

The relationship with time is dialogical. The apprehension of the past and the present bears witness to a conversation between death and survival. A final product of loss, the regeneration of the subject is possible at the site of the catastrophe. The survivors gather, with fervor or discouragement, the melancholic ruins of a collapsed humanity. This is the reason Cornelius decides to confront the images of the genocide.

Inside the parish, Cornelius saw for the first time the bones of the victims of the genocide. On two long tables, in a rectangular straw hut, human remains were exposed: skulls on the right and bones on the left.[5]

The refusal to bury the dead and the exposition of skeletons reinforces a memorial attitude in which the remains of the horror carry out an efficient work of interpellation and awareness. The display of dried bones provokes a violence that is painful to behold. It operates in counterpoint with the crystallizing of the poisonous fruit of hate. The inner struggle of characters like

Gérard mirrors this visible and concrete presence of the genocide at sites of memory. He escaped the killings by taking shelter under dead bodies:

I let the bodies of the first victims cover me up. But I was still half visible. Then I prayed very hard that others would fall beside me. . . . I had to swallow and spit their blood back out. . . . I could do nothing for them. . . . It would have been useless to resist. [6]

Piled up on one another, bodies become human shields. The omnipresence of blood seals an indestructible pact between the living and the dead. Experience is spattered with red, shame, and guilt. Gérard negotiates loss, grief, and survival. In everyday life post-genocide, the persistence of the past becomes a part of the collective identity. "After a story like that, anyway, everyone was a little dead," confides a character. In Derrida's terms, this conception of death is inseparable from survival.

Everything I say . . . about survival as a complication of the life/death opposition, comes from . . . an unconditional affirmation of life. . . . Survival is not what remains, but the most intense life possible. [7]

Grounded on an intensification of the desire for life in the face of adversity, *melancholia africana* allows for a cohabitation of the memory of genocide and alleviation from the affliction attached to this tragic event. Condemned to accept that he could reconstruct himself from what was destroyed, the survivor reconciles pain with relief. Hope and faith in better tomorrows are bound to sadness: "I need to believe that one can live with [the memory of genocide]. It rests my heart," says a protagonist. At first, Cornelius does not understand the relationship of interdependence that ties loss, mourning, and survival:

[He] couldn't even remember having seen on his walks the wounded and the mentally ill. On the contrary, the country was intact and people were settled into their daily lives. [8]

Further, he adds:

Thus, in the very country where death worked relentlessly to vanquish all energy, the force of life remained intact. [9]

The incomprehension stems from a dualist conception of life and death, of the present and the past. The behavior of survivors is not the result of a collective amnesia, being accustomed to adversity, nor a question of dignity. Those who survived explore the field of possibility, accepting the atrocities of the past. Conscious of the fact that they will never be able to change what happened, they also know that the construction of the future is incumbent upon them. Diop writes: "[Cornelius] knew it: accepting his past was the price to pay for beginning to find peace and a sense of the future." The past, the present, and the future are inscribed in a connectivity that is not sequential, but actional." [10] Death is evoked in a relational perspective oriented toward the actions of the living: "All this spilled blood must force us to recover," says a character. Edifying and redemptive, death indicates the continuity between the experience of the deceased and the destiny of the living: "The dead of Murambi dreamt too. . . . Their deepest desire was the resurrection of the living,"[11] affirms a protagonist. This pleonasm—the resurrection of the living—highlights the mental drama of those who, having escaped genocide, are tortured by guilt, resentment, fear, and doubt. They are victims more than survivors. The victim is passive. The victim becomes what she is subjected to. Her attitude affirms the victory of death. Essentially defined by her ability to separate what happened to her and who she is, the survivor never ceases to proclaim the superiority of life. To survive is to live forever. To live for oneself. To live for others. To live for those who remain present in us.

In *Le Passé devant soi*, Gilbert Gatore places the aftereffects of genocide at the heart of his novel. The work of this author, who was able to flee Rwanda at the time of the tragedy, draws on parallelism. Memory and forgetting. Cowardice and courage. Love and hate. The absurd and the quest for meaning. These dyads articulate infinitely throughout the paths of two characters: Isaro and Niko. Isaro is a young woman who escaped a fatal destiny. Although she was adopted and cared for wonderfully by her French parents, her story catches up to her one day while she is listening to the radio. From this moment, Isaro tries in vain to reconcile herself with her tumultuous past. Convinced that the site where existence ceased is where rebirth will be possible, she returns to her homeland and decides to compile the survivors' stories. Niko is a mute young man whose birth has the ring of mythic stories. Scorned and rejected because of his repulsive physical appearance, he lives a marginal life. By joining the "Enraged Volunteers," the suffering that he inflicted on the Other operates as a substitute for the suffering inflicted on him by his community. His participation in the massacres grants Niko a paradoxical existential validation. For the first time, he feels a sense of belonging. Assailed by shame and guilt, after the horror, he takes refuge in a cave that he shares with apes and the dead who have invaded his mind. The term "genocide" never appears in the story. Nor does it appear on the cover of the book: "Gilbert Gatore was born in 1981 in Rwanda. During the war, he began a journal that he had to leave behind." The paratext refers directly to the carnage of 1994. Why did he choose the word "war"? Instead of offering a critique of the writer for the words he chose not to say, his choice should be problematized.

Although the term "genocide" is entirely absent from the text, it functions as a narrative paradigm that the author deconstructs through a maximal descriptive device that refers to "massacres," to "work," to "machetes," to "bludgeons," to "executions," to "horror," to "cruelty," to "killings." The expressivity of detail is unambiguous. Genocide, genocide. . . . Does the absence of the keyword reflect the state of the discourse on this catastrophe to which no one holds the key? By refusing to name the unnamable, does the writer want us to "think the unthinkable"?[12] *Melancholia africana* appears here through discursive agony. Words are simultaneously practical, inappropriate, and frustrating. By directly naming a reality that is supposedly known to everyone, they tend to close the conversation before it has the chance to begin. Dividing those who disagree on meaning. Manipulating suffering in semantic contortions, instead of seeing one's own pain in the Other. This explains the competition of memories. The pain of some being more recognized than the pain of others, each group braces itself against a wall of words that divide, instead of reconciling their wounds. The flame of resentment and injustice ignites. It burns emotions buried in the oubliettes of a strangled memory.

In *Le Passé devant soi*, loss, mourning, and survival are rooted in agonizing and anxious language. The speech of the present emerges from a painful memory from which the broken subject must rebuild herself or complete her self-destruction: "It's anxiety, in the end, that in unifying the past and the present, situates them in relation to the other and gives them a community of meaning."[13] Anxiety carries characters and readers into "zones of non-being," forcing them to "live the unlivable." It flays good intentions and pious vows by mauling the angelic image of the self. It forces the individual to abandon the virtuous mask she wears by observing from afar a catastrophe from which she wrongly believes herself exempt. We confine the monster to an exclusive alterity. We are afraid of recognizing ourselves in her. *Melancholia africana* embraces her purulent humanity through involuntary empathy. Whether we like it or not, because of what the monster inflicted upon us, she becomes a part of us. In the context of the Rwandan genocide, we are constrained to consider the collapse of supreme values through a "teleological suspension of ethics,"[14] a suspension possible through the ethnicization of national identity that makes no sense unless the minority group is completely wiped out. Hate and dehumanization of the Other become a catalyst for the establishment of a new political order. The codes and laws that guarantee the cohesion of the state no longer apply to a part of the population considered to be the enemy within that must be exterminated. Rwandan citizens of Tutsi origin can no longer call upon the principles regulating action and moral conduct, foundational of the polis. Facing this situation, what tools do the writer and the individual have at their disposal to continue promoting the human being?

In Gilbert Gatore's work, the "teleological suspension of ethics" emerges in an intimate space assailed by a series of provocative and disturbing thoughts:

What should be done when resistance, even by the sacrifice of self, cannot save anything nor anyone? Does the hand of the one who kills in this way have other motives to kill other than to preserve?

Why does the victim obey his executioner even when he knows that he has no chance of escaping? [15]

When the victim follows the instructions given to him, maybe the entire responsibility should be given to the executioner. . . . To obey, to leave the executioner in his crime until the end. . . . Obedience as a sign of the inexorability of hope, the final hold in hopeless situations. . . . Humans hope even when death is certain. . . . [16]

Does the instinct of survival justify killing? [17]

In some cases, there is no choice between accepting and refusing horror, collaborating or distancing oneself from it, but being on the side of those who commit it or those who suffer it. [18]

Can a murderer go back to his life from before? . . . Does taking someone's life forbid having one's own? [19]

Is murder unpardonable because the only person from whom pardon could come is no longer there? [20]

Measured by the extent of the invalidation of ethics, these quotes are symptomatic of a discursive agony that unveils unseemly and hurtful truths. The novelist struggles with "the distress of explanation that comes from the fact that we must describe and elucidate a negative phenomenon, not as the decomposition of a positive phenomenon . . . but, in itself, in its specific constitution that has the profile of an erratic and paroxystic event." [21] This distress of explanation exposes the deficiencies of theological, moralizing, or Manichean rhetoric that pits sinners against saints, good against evil, and reason against madness. It forces us to leave behind conventional dichotomies that prevent us from confronting the dark side of the human being, this shadow side, that when it comes to light, reveals supreme horror. Loss, grief, and survival go beyond good and evil to handle absurd truths. These three steps take place through the examination of the atrocities of national history that contaminate personal history. Although the judgment and condemnation of the culprit are fundamental, they cannot diminish the importance of individual and collective work. This work leads to the reinvention of new modes of life, born out of the failure of ideals and values that previously organized the existence of populations that genocide—a pathological form of nationalism—divided into killers and victims.

Thwarted hope pierces the confines of the intimate to resolve a public tragedy in private. Niko and Isaro are constantly taking a journey into themselves. They try to pacify an inner space tormented by the unspeakable. Subjected to the throes of a painful and recalcitrant memory, they live with the aftereffects of a tragic event that compels the individual to negotiate an existential scar. Is this scar a stoic memory of pain? An inoffensive mark left by a wound after healing? Physical or mnestic trace bearing witness to moral suffering? Paradoxically, the scar highlights the ending of something that remains. This enduring imprint on the body and the mind appears through a dialectic of perpetual questioning and reflection. Because genocide destroyed "a world of human relations, issued from speech and action, that in themselves are endless,"[22] the work of introspection makes an aporetic reconciliation possible. Whether victim or killer, the harmony of the subject with herself or the Other is contaminated by relational vulnerability related to the original disaster. However, this situation does not put healing in peril. By exercising an ethical pressure that operates as a means of coercion, it forces individuals to no longer cross the line of no return.

The tension between the exploration of the intimate and the excavation of History deconstructs traditional modes of identification. It goes beyond habitual emotions: sadness, empathy, compassion, pity that one feels toward the victim, anger, contempt, and rejection of the killer. In this type of configuration, the opposition between good and evil paralyzes becoming. Subjectivity is petrified by the History that distributes irreducible roles that cannot be overcome. By problematizing the figure of the victim and the killer, I affirm that "Evil" is also "a possibility that is only opened by the encounter with Good."[23] Without confusing them, *melancholia africana* requires us to look differently at the antinomic couples born out of violence that creates by destroying and destroys by creating. This utopian perspective bears witness to an "aptitude to open a breach in the density of the real."[24] It could blind some, cause a legitimate irritability in others, and reassure those to whom we never extend our hand. In any case, it has the merit of destabilizing certainties. Perhaps this perspective moves prudently toward the question of for/giving?

NOTES

1. This concept was developed by Mahmood Mamdani. For this professor of political science and anthropology, the pornography of violence is a free and disproportionate display of violence that accentuates the divide between those who commit it and those who observe it. It is characterized by a total absence of social, historical, or political contextualization. Televisual voyeurism puts on the pretense of virtuous and humanitarian denunciation. Instead of focusing on the humanitarian emergency, it would be best to place emphasis on political solutions. In the long term, only they will put a stop to the postcolonial absurdities that manifest themselves through the unending spectacle of famine, poverty, and violence.

2. Boubacar Boris Diop, *Murambi, le livre des ossements*, Paris, Zulma, 2011.

3. Gilbert Gatore, *Le Passé devant soi: figures de la vie impossible*, vol. 1, Paris, Phébus, 2008.

4. Boubacar Boris Diop, *Murambi*, p. 62.

5. *Ibid.*, p. 97.

6. *Ibid.*, p. 224–227.

7. Jacques Derrida, *Apprendre à vivre enfin*, Paris, Galilée/Le Monde, 2005, p. 53–54.

8. Boubacar Boris Diop, *Murambi*, p. 69.

9. *Ibid.*, p. 213.

10. Time has no value until the moment when the individual transforms what is by her actions.

11. Boubacar Boris Diop, *Murambi*, p. 234.

12. Fabien Eboussi Boulaga, "Penser l'impensable," *Le Génocide Rwandais: les interrogations des intellectuels africains*, Yaoundé, Éditions Clé, 2006, p. 63.

13. Michel Foucault, *Maladie mentale et psychologie*, p. 50.

14. Søren Kierkegaard, *"Fear and Trembling"* and *"Repetition,"* translated by Howard V. Hong and Edna H. Hong, Princeton, NJ, Princeton University Press, 1983.

15. Gilbert Gatore, *Le Passé devant soi: figures de la vie impossible*, p. 155–156.

16. *Ibid.*

17. *Ibid.*

18. *Ibid.*, p. 159.

19. *Ibid.*, p. 166.

20. *Ibid.*, p. 169.

21. Fabien Eboussi Boulaga, "Penser l'impensable," p. 67.

22. Hannah Arendt, *Qu'est-ce que la politique?*, Paris, Éditions du Seuil, 1995, p. 135.

23. Alain Badiou, *L'éthique: essai sur la conscience du mal*, p. 79.

24. Paul Ricœur, *L'idéologie et l'utopie*, Paris, Éditions du Seuil, 1997, p. 405.

Chapter Seven

From the Gaze of the Other to Self-Reflection

I am invisible, understand, simply because people refuse to see me. . . . When they approach me they see only my surroundings, themselves or figments of their imagination, indeed, everything and anything except me.
—Ralph Ellison

He who starts behind in a race must forever remain behind or run faster than the man in the front. . . . It is a call to do the impossible. It is enough to cause the Negro to give up in despair. And yet, there are times when life demands the perpetual doing of the impossible.
—Martin Luther King Jr.

In the postcolonial context, *melancholia africana* takes an interest in the dynamics of daily survival of oppressed populations. Populations qualified as passive or resigned because they take paths of resistance that do not respond to the criteria of others. Populations that advance at a rhythm that others consider too slow. There are currently adults who are older than the supposedly independent African state. After over fifty years of existence on an IV, many would like us to accomplish what was realized elsewhere in several centuries. Instead of confining ourselves to sterile imitation, we should examine the specificity of our conditions of existence and provide responses adapted to the tensions inherent to our historical becoming. By applying frameworks of interpretation elaborated by the Other, we hope to copy their Euromodernity, which is ineffective in our countries. Our identity is trapped in the Western gaze and distinguishes itself from it in an essentialist manner or by claiming universality by default. For nearly five decades, we have been trying to establish relations of exchange by reproducing imported economic, political, and cultural models. Many leaders also manipulate authenticity and traditions to legitimize abuses of power, dictatorship, mismanagement, and neocolonialism. Traitors, collaborators, and bandits have always existed. We must unmask them and drive them out.

Very much in fashion in recent years, globalization fell in our laps several centuries ago when European slavery and colonialism landed on the continent. Can we celebrate it in the same way because we are living in the twenty-first century? Let's accept that we did not negotiate the conditions of our presence in the supposed global village and act accordingly. Established on the foundation of historical domination, globalization reinforces the separation between those who have it all and those who have nothing. Poverty has become the blinding symbol of Africa's non-participation in the concert of benefits that the globalized third millennium has to offer. Poverty calls us back to elementary issues—not very postcolonial—more or less trivial in other places: potable water, hygiene, daily meals, health, and education. If globalization exists, it is that of Africa on its knees. The obscene spectacle of our children adopted by Hollywood. Our daughters with torn hymens. Our sisters with vulvas beaded with sorrow who sell distress on European asphalt. Our presidents for life. Our human butchery in suffering minor. Thrown to the lions, our floods of despair are visible on the big screen in Times Square or in French households. Seen from afar, Africa is outside of the world. The apocalypse every day. The reflection of a simulated reality where everything goes from bad to worse. Philanthropy prospers in the fields of pain. Charity replaces justice. Humanitarian determination is a substitute for political responsibility. The special effects of misery and violence obsess spectators. Victims of compassion devoid of respect, recalling the Zoe's Ark controversy,[1] their relationship with Africa belongs to the realm of fantasized altruism, pity, horror, disgust, and contempt. Apparently, in this part of the world, people kill each other for no reason, and die, every five minutes, of hunger, AIDS, or malaria.

After having complained about the past presence of the Other, they beg them for help and cozy up with friends from China. Their leaders are tragicomic clowns. The populations are the spectators and the actors in their own tragedy. Never any good news, only slaughter. One cannot help but wonder how we continue to be creative, to live, to be born, to die, to laugh, to cry, to play, to sing, to dance, to make love, and to aspire to happiness like everyone else . . .

James Baldwin states that a day will come when the Black can no longer accuse the white. The writer invites his community to prepare for this inevitable moment that will come peacefully, or with violence. Those who cannot prepare themselves, he says, always perish.[2] It is less a question of clearing the oppressor of their responsibility than reclaiming the inventiveness that the oppressed must bring into their existence in order to free themselves. The urgency of our condition requires us to stop asking of others what we should accomplish ourselves. At the beginning of the historical fraud, covering ourselves with the coat of innocence and naiveté allowed us to name the unnamable. Swallowing the pill of life without tomorrow. To survive the chaos and the loss. It has been more than thirty years since Baldwin left us. Has the day he predicted come? Are we ready to confront it? Have we already perished? The bell of indictment has rung. We often complain about the gaze, the non-intervention of the Other, and atrocities committed against us. We impute the whole of our woes to them. We also believe if whites were to exercise good will, they could improve our condition in seven days. After slavery and colonization, shouldn't we change our tune? Create a new music? Have we developed a "dependency complex"?[3] Why do we expect everything from the Other and nothing from ourselves? Incapable of planning our becoming, we confess a desire for eternal servitude. Unconsciously, we allocate the responsibility of our destiny to the Other, thus signing our own death sentence.

In the arts, some venture to talk about a world literature in French or world music through which we would slip our contribution "to the meeting of giving and receiving."[4] The black diamonds that float in the great blue; African lives incinerated in Parisian buildings; Yaguine Koita and Fode Tounkara dead in the landing gear compartment of a plane to Brussels, the one-way charters for Bamako; Amadou Diallo, riddled with bullets by the New York City police; sub-Saharan workers assaulted in Italy; undocumented migrants besieging churches. . . . All of this brings me violently back to our globalization by default. It continually confirms the excluded and shirking status that we have carried around since 1492. The supposed freedom of movement finds its coherence in a frenzied desire to flee poverty. A desire shared by the intellectual elite reduced to vagrancy, the middle class petrified in the bare minimum, and the lumpenproletariat in agony. Anchored in a position of lacking, our choices are not choices. Confronted with problems of existential insecurity related to employment, housing, health, and education, we are now slaves to the precariousness of our living conditions.

"To free ourselves" from colonial power does not imply equal opportunity nor a common destiny. The freedom of the postcolonial subject affirms itself in spaces of social death. Those who are able rush into the Western Elsewhere, the only possible escape. . . . Elsewhere, where the repression of anger, tears, and aspirations are clothed in pretenses. Condemned to bury a part of our humanity in order to survive, perhaps we should admit, with Frieda Ekotto, that we are "false global subjects"[5] in a state of permanent peril. Rather than moping around, we need to take our responsibility by examining the nudity of our existence. The politics of respectability that would oblige the African thinker to denounce or counter racist discourses and the negative images that the West propagates about Africa do not concern me. Let the negrophobic negrologists keep explaining to Europe why Africa is dying. They certainly hear the cry of the African, but do they understand it? The obsessive and alienating gaze that the Other inflicts on us is in their eye. It belongs to them. Why should we misrecognize ourselves in their mirror? Africa, museum of horrors. Anomaly of modernity. Abyss of all vices. Temple of endless despair. Fertile ground for toxic humanitarianism. This Africa is not mine. Africa caress. Africa sadness. Africa atrocity. Africa beauty. Africa gaiety.

Our socio-economic and political configurations are outside the chronology of all those who hear our cries without understanding them. The time has come to look back at ourselves, avoiding the narcissism that would reproduce racial hierarchization. Attributing qualitative semantics to cutaneous difference reduces the Other to nothing. It is no longer a question of being Black, beautiful, proud, and strong in response to those who for centuries covered our souls with sins, fears, terrors, and tragedies. Black, beautiful, proud, and strong because they continue to profane our interiority. Black, beautiful, proud, and strong because we were ashamed, are still ashamed? Ashamed to be so ugly, so Black, so weak, so naked, so impure, "[having] no ontological resistance in the eyes of the white man."[6] Through these supposed qualities—whiteness, beauty, purity, pride, and power—they strove to destroy our integrity. Beyond the economic aspect, the civilizing mission, the slave trade, slavery, and colonization bear witness to a love of self out of control. The edification of the self turns out to be impossible without the destruction of the Other. By creating the *Nègre*, the white man grasped alterity as an ability to demolish the human being standing in front of him. Paradoxically, this demolition comes with an obsession to assimilate. While allowing France to respond to the obligations of its ideals, assimilationist politics put the Black into a prison without exit. In order to be recognized by the Other, she must hate and deny what she is. Despite the work of acculturation and alienation, she remains a *Nègre* before the white. She will never become that Other. The irreducibility of this realization is a wake-up call. Deprived of the I of their identity, the idea of a Black self exists through the discourse of the Other on the self. "I am the history of the rejection of who I am."[7] Why should we strive to adopt an image whose light covers us up with darkness? As a human being, the Black "can have the representation 'I.'"[8] According to Immanuel Kant, this ability "raises him infinitely above all the other beings on earth. By this he is a *person* . . . that is, a being altogether different in rank and dignity from *things*, such as irrational animals, with which one may deal and dispose at one's discretion."[9]

Afrocentric researchers work toward this process of repossessing the self. They proclaim the nobility of our origins and elaborate on the scientific and cultural heritage of Kemet. They also speak on the monstrosity of those who dehumanized their ancestors. The physical/psychological collision between the Black and the white transformed skin color into an explosive discursive surface on which values, qualities, defects, lacks, and achievements clash. Despite the fluidity of time, relational dissymmetry persists. We paddle blithely through nonsense. The nights of yesterday continue to oppress the new day. Destroying the master's house with his tools, we do not mend injustice. Revenge and vengeance liberate no one. They simply invert the relation of power through an identical destructive dynamic. Exploring the dark corners of our mutual destiny will unveil our mutilated interiority. White and Black, what is our relationship with History? The narration of egocentric progress and the experience of unspeakable catastrophe. Reconstruction/memory of a glorious past and destruction/forgetting of a dishonorable period. Thunderous cries of joy and voiceless moans. Some possess History, others were dispossessed of it. In a world where we are condemned to live together, we should perhaps reconcile our antinomies by deconstructing a History trapped in victory and defeat, good and evil, innocence and guilt. Dualism—victim versus oppressor—endlessly masks what brings us together by solidifying negative alterity. Beyond the centuries-old role playing, the original encounter produced a shared vulnerability that has grown over time. Superficial impassivity and denial of suffering shown by the West reveals a visceral fear. A fear that we experience when we must confront the dark side of the human. Lying becomes an act of good faith "by means of avoidance,"[10] a survival tactic that sublimates the criminal reality that we have created and that we have been living in for centuries. What should we make of the fundamental texts that exalt values and ideals consubstantial with our existence? Can we read them in light of what they have engendered, accompanied, forgotten/refused to denounce? Has reason gone to bed with the unreasonable? How can we unmask the monster within us? In recognizing it, we chip away at the heritage upon which self-esteem was established. The fictive innocence that veils the original horror disappears. Terror settles in. How can one abandon one's pride and take responsibility for one's actions? An essential universe of reference collapses. In this simultaneously porous, terrifying, and promising space, the dominators and the dominated will be in a position to cope with History's madness.

Although it is beyond understanding, this madness calls for reflection, prudence, and humility. Thanks to it, we remain alert to the monstrous potential within us all.[11] We recognize the absolute superiority of life, accept the omnipresence of the *I don't know*, of psychological castration, of question marks and ellipses. We think critically about the common destiny that historical antecedents mangled. A terrifying crossing through areas of uncertainty and anxiety, retrospective analysis leads to ambiguous relief. The defeat of ethics and the supposed victory of evil over good will never be able to explain the unexplainable. Resorting to principles considered to be universal does not impede divergent readings of a shared History. They will never constrain the oppressed to adopt the point of view of the oppressors. The sacralization of a set of ideals that have manifestly failed requires us to question them. Instead of considering them dogmas that fall under common sense, we should situate them in the mechanisms of the exercise of power. In this context, human rights, humanism, reason, truth, good, evil, love, happiness, reason, freedom, equality, fraternity, and progress are elements of a variable geometry submitted to a project of domination. In a Eurocentric semantics that racializes belonging to the human family, the universal confuses alterity with exclusion from the outset. It then pretends to end exclusion by means of a coercive mimeticism. The Other must become like us. Yet, if they "succeed," we no longer exist. It is through this both totalitarian and restricted vision that the African will enter into a universal space that works to annihilate difference to better solidify it. Valuing the white goes along with devaluing the Black. The original narcissism provoked a belligerent narcissism in certain descendants of slaves and colonized peoples who express or sometimes stifle a desire for revenge. In response to this state of mind, the hurt oppressors drown in self-accusation. They want to redeem their wounded ego. The arrogant tormentors detach themselves from the abomination and engage in an active practice of forgetting. Yet, "forgetfulness is already a form of guilt."[12] Refusal to examine a troubled past sincerely does not contribute to its disappearance.

My work is a form of *parrhesia*, or "the courage of truth in the one who speaks and takes the risk of saying, despite everything, all the truth that he thinks, but also the courage of the interlocutor who accepts to take the painful truth he hears as true."[13] My aim is to establish a new pact of mutual comprehension. To put an end to the atemporal partition that plays out between the tormentor and the tormented: "One is distorted as an oppressor . . . only preoccupied with his privileges, of their defense at all cost; the other as oppressed, broken in his development, complacent in his own defeat."[14] The role-playing has gone on for too long. It isolates subjectivity, preceding the arrival of actors in the world, and surviving their death. How can we get out of this hellish immobility? The challenge of the present world and the world to come revolves around the invention of new relational modes. We must detach ourselves from old zones of comfort/discomfort that reproduce negative alterity. The encounter will happen when we will have all overcome our prejudices. A figure born out of centuries of nonsense, a dialogue between the victim and the killer, powerlessness and power in which neither side listened, led to an alienating paralysis. When will we give to the Other what we wanted to obtain from them? Blacks and whites are forced "to tell the truth, accepting voluntarily and explicitly that this telling of the truth could cost them their own existence."[15] Taking the risk is liberating. It stops us from legitimizing the oppression or from avenging the abominations of the past. The physical/psychological collision continues to determine the relationship with the self and the Other. The majority of Westerners do not want to answer for the crimes of their ancestors. They have developed defense mechanisms that allow them to remove themselves, as individuals, from this part of History. Objectively, they were neither slave traders, nor plantation owners, nor colonizers. However, the profit resulting from these capitalist ventures contributed to an economic prosperity that continues to benefit them. The sub-Saharan and the people of African descent find themselves prisoners of a condition inherent to the initial catastrophe. When they "extricate themselves" from it, they take on a new identity, that of the different or exceptional Black.

Centuries of dysfunctional dependence, accumulated anxiety, and undeclared desire forbid a peaceful common becoming. The exploration of our disarmed humanity will introduce inventiveness in History. Only this exploration will allow for the creation of a new language where I and you exist in a relationship of reciprocity that gives birth to the *we*. Let's embrace the "ugly beauty"[16] of a relationship where destruction and creation are knotted together in the *cœurs à corps* that destabilize the certainties of the conquerors by tending to the uncertainties of the defeated. If we invite the Other to take a journey within our fear, we give the future a chance. Diminishing the Other does not raise me up. The whites of today are not guilty of the crimes committed by their ancestors. Many are, however, guilty of continuing those crimes. Inheritors of an ideology that trampled a set of populations and a wealth soiled by Negro tears, they must examine their relationship with History. Critical thinking will help repair what was destroyed. If they refuse, we must move on without them. Reparation is not only economic, but also human. "For ourselves and for humanity . . . we must make a new start, develop a new way of thinking, and endeavor to create a new man."[17]

Confined in a system of representation, "the black is a black man; that is, as a result of a series of aberrations of affect, he is rooted at the core of a universe from which he must be extricated."[18] The subject embroiders her future on the canvas of interiority. The enemy and the darkness are within us. The ally and the light as well. To resolve this impasse, we must fight within ourselves, not against the Other. How can we come toward the self to better open ourselves to the Other? How do we live? Who are we? Where are we going? How do we manage our daily life? What are the strategies of survival that poeticize adversity? What should we do with this being in the world born out of a complication between heroism and defeatism, hope and despair, dream and nightmare? What color is the Black?

NOTES

1. Zoe's Ark is French charity organization that was involved in a scandal in Chad in 2007. While claiming to rescue orphans from Darfur, taking them to be fostered in France, they were

convicted of 103 counts of child abduction. Most of the children were found to be Chadian, with one or more living parent or guardian.

2. *The James Baldwin Anthology*. Clair Burch, Christopher Sorrenti. DVD. Act and Educational Media, 2008.

3. Aimé Césaire, *Discourse on Colonialism*, p. 59.

4. African authors and professors who are published and rewarded in Paris, New York, and London are often inaccessible on the continent. The geographical positioning defined by these situational variables related to questions of literary, economic, and sometimes political survival condition the (non) reception of their works in the territory of origin. People no longer question whether cinema and literature produced on the outside have a role to play there. For whom do these artists create? For whom do the researchers write? This question has become completely superfluous, outdated, and borderline insulting. Many claim to belong to a global world where they only exist by closing themselves off in the local. The Other transforms constantly into the spokesperson of an Africa that they aim to distance themselves from.

5. Frieda Ekotto, "La Mondialisation, l'immigration et le cinéma africain d'expression française, pour un devenir moderne," *Nouvelles Études Francophones*, vol. 24, no. 1, Spring 2009. In this article, Ekotto explains how with illegal immigration and globalization, the Black is reduced to slavery and maintained in servile conditions. She focuses on the exploitation of African bodies through the figure of the immigrant who, in fleeing misery, brushes with/is subjected to death or imprisonment in refugee camps. It is worth studying the businesses that prosper thanks to perfectly polished systems of exploitation. They employ immigrants without documents without declaring them or paying them fairly. Industries such as restaurants, cleaning and building companies are a bottomless reservoir of cheap labor subjected to injustice.

6. Frantz Fanon, *Black Skin, White Masks*, p. 110.

7. June Jordan, "Poem about My Rights," *Directed by Desire: The Collected Poems of June Jordan*, Port Townsend, WA, Copper Canyon Press, 2005, p. 311.

8. Immanuel Kant, *Lectures on Anthropology*, eds. A. Wood and R. Louden, Cambridge, Cambridge University Press, 2013, p. 127.

9. *Ibid.*

10. Sigmund Freud, *Métapsychologie*, Paris, Gallimard, Folio essais, 1968, p. 62.

11. History has shown that the victims of the past have often transformed into the oppressors of the present. See the work by Mahmood Mamdani on this question: *When Victims Become Killers: Colonialism, Nativism and the Genocide in Rwanda*, Princeton, NJ, Princeton University Press, 2001, and "Making Sense of Political Violence in Postcolonial Africa," *Identity, Culture, and Politics*, vol. 3, no. 2, December 2002. To make sense of violence, the researcher suggests examining the process by which the victim and the oppressor constitute polarized identity groups. How do those who commit violence define themselves? How do they define those on whom they inflict it? Mamdani also invites a denaturalization of race, ethnicity, and religion. Although they are factors of division, these three characteristics become coherent in the organization and exercise of power. The tragic events that occurred in South Africa in 2008 showed how the old victims of Apartheid launched a murderous campaign. Populations, out of breath and exasperated by the atrocity of their life conditions, exhorted foreigners, Africans/Blacks, to leave their country by using unnamable violence. Just because one has survived a particularly painful experience does not mean that one will not inflict it on others. Victim status does not necessarily lead to a natural inclination to virtue.

12. Theodor W. Adorno, *Can One Live After Auschwitz? A Philosophical Reader*, Stanford, CA, Stanford University Press, 2003, p. 437.

13. Michel Foucault, *Le Courage de la vérité: Le gouvernement de soi et des autres II*, Paris, Éditions des Hautes Études en Science Sociales, Gallimard, Éditions du Seuil, 2009, p. 14.

14. Albert Memmi, *Portrait du colonisé, Portrait du colonisateur*, Paris, Gallimard, "Folio," 1985, p. 108.

15. Michel Foucault, *Le Courage de la vérité: Le gouvernement de soi et des autres*, p. 56.

16. "Ugly Beauty," Thelonious Monk, on the album *Underground*, Columbia, 1968.

17. Frantz Fanon, *The Wretched of the Earth*, translated by Richard Philcox, with commentary by Jean-Paul Sartre and Homi K. Bhabha, New York, Grove Press, 1964, p. 239.

18. Frantz Fanon, *Black Skin, White Masks*, p. 8.

Chapter Eight

"On va faire comment?":
Fact of Language, Civic Renunciation,
or Theodicy of the Everyday
in the Postcolony

Existence in a banana republic, what a calamitous destiny.
—Mongo Beti

It has been going on for more than fifty years, is there any reason it should stop? Yes, one, things must change.
—Jean Léopold Dominique

A society that drives its members to desperate solutions is a nonviable society, a society that must be replaced. The citizen's duty is to say it.
—Frantz Fanon

The exploration of the Cameroonian expression *"on va faire comment?"* (literally, "how are we going to do?") will allow for some self-reflection, revealing a complexity that often goes unnoticed. Tracing the origins of this phrase that punctuates daily life in Douala and Yaoundé is not my aim. Instead, we will see how Cameroonians resist their surrounding malaise with aggressive and tragicomic tenacity. The expressivity of their resistance emerges from a situation where fatality has been transformed into psychological pragmatics.

The question is commonly used to mark irony, grief, compassion, and surrendering to the status quo. We deplore injustice, abuses of power, and the absence of ethics while proclaiming the impossibility of doing anything about it. The conjunction of the verbs *faire* (to do) and *aller* (to go), connected to the adverb *comment* (how), apparently emphasizes possible modes of action. Despite its violative and reactive potentiality, the question calls for no response on the level of action. Passivity, moral and intellectual lassitude are the quintessence of the expression. In such a context, to question is to resign oneself: "linguistic exchanges are also relations of symbolic power in which power relations are realized"[1] between powerless citizens and the state that intimidates them by using its "repressive apparatus."[2] The conditions of enunciation comfort the speaker and the receiver in resignation coated in the gloss of empathy. Achille Mbembe explains how the postcolonial system creates and uses language and signs to convert the oppressive space into a perverse relational space. The subjugated people contribute to the perpetuation of the tyranny that victimizes them. According to the historian and political philosopher, a form of "conviviality" and "intimacy" develops. The oppressors and the oppressed establish relationships of connivance by "playing" with the domination.[3] The episodic surges in violence do not result in shifts of political power. The opposition surfs on the people's discontent without conceiving of an efficient plan of civic action. The lack of synergy between citizens' anger, the political class, and the intelligentsia reinforces stagnation, or regression.

In February 2008, there were "hunger riots" in a country of "food self-sufficiency." A revolt of youth infuriated by their restless wandering, or a fraud orchestrated by "sorcerers' apprentices"? Joe's imprisoned conscience cries out in the wilderness.[4] Valséro raps about the amputated heroism of a scorned youth: "I live in Yaoundé, you talk about a life. . . . More like death . . . this country kills its kids . . . the youth are dyin' a slow death . . . we're hustlin' hard, but there ain't nothing we can do. . . . We been in pain too long, and still in pain, please a breath of air." Legitimate anger dies out in favor of looting. In the name of a call to order, bullets from the brutish infantry fire through the indignation. Disengagement with the *res publica* determines the ethos.[5] The public matter is oligarchy. The citizen submits to this "privatization of power."[6] Weary of their fruitless efforts, they shrug their shoulders or let out a sardonic laugh, asking: "*on va faire comment?*" This expresses their obedience to an unjust order, their distress, and their vague and erratic desire for freedom. A verbalization of a mechanism of self-defense, "*on va faire comment?*" is a concrete response to a real malaise. Pessimism and disenchantment culminate in a *government of self* that encourages the death of civic hope.[7] Cameroonians no longer believe in revolutions, in politicians, or elections. Politics is senseless. They have known the music since 1958.[8]

The question, which conveys the inertia and resignation in civic life, constitutes an essential verse in the book of survival. Prisoners of chaotic living conditions, encouraged by a republic that is present *in absentia*, Cameroonians have developed a situational way of being. "*On va faire comment?*"

is a mantra. In Buddhism and Hinduism, a mantra is a holy phrase with spiritual power. According to its Sanskrit etymology, it means "instrument of thought." By attributing this meaning to the question, we remark that it reveals a theodicy of the everyday. In their practice of daily life, Cameroonians tame their environment. *"On va faire comment?"* is the "cunning of reason" confronted with the irrational. Submitted to misfortune and suffering, the subject develops an ethic of self that regulates her relation with nonsense. Célestin Monga notes that "many Africans of all social backgrounds [cultivate] . . . skepticism as well as an inconsolable melancholy. This does not prevent them from surviving anguish, rejecting suicide."[9] Existence is understood as a profession of faith. A devotion submitted to abnegation and frustration. The individual leans on modest joys, little pleasures, and the desire to live her life because, after all, she only has one.

Civic suicide is indissociable from individual responsibility in the private sphere. This indissociably gives birth to a "metaphysics of improvisation" that unfolds through "a creative realism"[10] and "parades of survival."[11] Thanks to this poetic disposition toward adversity, the individual conquers her environment. She flounders in a socioeconomic space where the law of the arbitrary and of "every man for himself" act as *modus vivendi*. The failure of the state produced a set of ideas, beliefs, and ways of being that, while encouraging strategies of survival in the short term, promote the disappearance of a sense of civic-mindedness in the long term. Echoing weary voices treading the road of resistance, *"on va faire comment?"* is a solemn acceptance of civic powerlessness. The Cameroonian sees herself in a mirror reflecting the everyday Sisyphus and the fearful citizen closing her eyes. Accustomed to impulse reduced to nothing, she fears retaliation. Submission reflects a blinding image. The citizen can no longer open her eyes. She gouges them out. In the unbearable night, she decides to be done with it. Hara-kiri. The citizen is dead! Long live the citizen! Has she ever existed? Yes. Until 1958, she participated in the nationalist struggle. Between 1960 and 1990, she was imprisoned. Stifled. Traumatized. Intimidated. Misled. Tortured. Lobotomized. Exiled. Sometimes killed. Fed from the bottle of fear, silence, and self-destructive values, she survives. Lulled by the deafening purr of despotism, she is slowly dying. In 1991, the citizen was reborn from her ashes. She fought for democracy. Unfortunately, it was rigged, manipulated, and corrupt. The civic spirit transforms into a carcass with a fatal stench. The ghosts of murdered combatants wander through kneeling consciences. Buried in tombs of anonymity and forgetting, all those who died so that we could live shed blue tears on a dozing posterity. *Comme-mes-morts-action!*[12]

Whether they are partisans of the ruling power or the opposition, politicians are jokers that no one finds funny anymore. Free beer at the next electoral joke, the populations will drink. No matter who pays. T-shirts and hats with portraits of any knucklehead, they'll wear with pride. After all, it's the country's money. Victims of a number of castrating codes and treatments, Cameroonians have become docile, sometimes cynical citizens. They demand the right to civic resignation. Can we hold it against them? They are playing the game of nonsense, hoping for a happy life. They are discharging their duties to a moribund country. Conscious of their belonging to a disorganized political community, they brace themselves in the private sphere, the only guarantee of satisfaction. After all, the affection of one's partner or the smiles and tears of a baby are a language that recall the fundamentals of existence: love and selflessness. Preoccupied by the well-being of their children and extended family, Cameroonians do their best to be excellent parents. They bleed themselves dry to pay for medical expenses, school uniforms, books, meals, and that little bit extra to delight their loved ones. Waking up early and going to bed late, they drive taxis, *bend-skin,*[13] roam as street vendors with products piled up on their arms, shoulders, and head. At the market, sitting behind their stalls, Cameroonians work without respite. Others are nurses, barbers, mechanics, masons, *pousseurs,*[14] walking vendors, plumbers, teachers, housekeepers, farmers. Some tap into schemes for quick money: prostitution, Internet marriage, traffic, and crimes of all sorts that prosper everywhere where misery, neglect, and wandering cast a shadow over life. Many also fall back on ethnic, religious, or community organizations. They latch onto the prophecy of the everyday.

Out of the sight of a Republic that is celebrating fifty years of collective asphyxia, the docile and cynical citizen spills blue on existence: "driven back to the need for survival . . . [have they] lost the ability to project themselves into history?"[15] The more it changes, the more it stays the same. Time goes by. Nothing happens. We move forward only to better move back. Everything is fine, except the rest. Memory and forgetting are twin sisters separated by feelings. Have the elders lost their memory? Maybe they manipulate it to avoid taking responsibility? A father does not cry in front of his daughter. . . . Is his boy able to bear his tears? He will never beget his father. How could a generation that received so much leave a failing inheritance to the children that they pretend to love?

"On va faire comment?"

When people asking this question recognize it as performative speech, *"on va faire comment?"* will prompt empowerment, and the ability to realize an act by speaking it. The subject might find the strength and courage to act in the *polis*. For now, *"On va faire comment?"* is a veiled way of saying both "yes" and "no."

History shows that civic combat has never ended in the victory of the general will. Cameroonians have chosen to abandon themselves to survival. Here, survival is often learning to die. To die from that insidious, mocking, and slow death that shows itself in the abandonment of political action: "with the diminishing of the power to act, felt as a diminishing of the effort to exist, comes the true reign of suffering."[16]

"On va faire comment?" contributes to a process of collective zombification. To live a life marked by pragmatic fatalism is but the illusion of existence. We are, in reality, empty people. We talk because our mouths are open. Lips and a tongue that move without words to convey meaning, rebirth, or knowledge. We breathe because we have a beating heart instead of feeling the emotions brought on by the fundamental breath. Sacrificing frustrated citizenship on the altar of short-term survival endangers the destiny of an entire people. The heroism of the everyday reflects life on credit. At our death, our children will inherit a heavy debt that they will pay at a great cost while cursing us. This heroism of life on credit invites us to question our modes of resistance: "A moment comes when tenacity becomes morbid perseverance. Hope is no longer the open door to the future, but to the illogical maintenance of an subjective attitude in organized divorce with the real."[17]

Although the subjectivity of this wounded people has broken with the absent state, the reality of their condition remains implacable. What is a citizen? Does this term not evoke the energy of personal engagement in the political arena, for the good of oneself and others? Does owning a national identity card or a passport mean that we deserve that title? Is it a symbol of belonging without substance? Isn't being a citizen to aspire in the depths of one's being to influence one's destiny and that of the people by being active in the *polis*? Doesn't the rejection of an oppressive reality work toward the construction of a better world? At the heart of darkness, there is light. How can we rekindle the flame of desire extinguished by decades of frustration? The frustration of unfulfilled desire. When the subject's request is denied, shouldn't this lack, this incompleteness, make her strive to fulfill it, rather than putting up with its denial? Isn't frustration supposed to multiply the strength of desire to the point of obsession? In our country of Cameroon, it often leads to the peaceful lassitude of intrepid fatalism. How can we remedy this strange mix of heroism and defeatism? How can we understand that it is when struggling in extreme situations that "man experiences limits that are directly the conditions of his freedom and the foundation of his actions"?[18]

Omnipresent among nationalist combatants and the major figures of Black liberation in the era of Jim Crow and the Ku Klux Klan, civic desire transformed pariahs into citizens, slaves and colonized people into free men and women. This, before the U.S. constitution legally granted them that status. Citizens because they wanted to be citizens. Citizens because they were conscious of their rights, duties, and responsibilities toward their people. Citizens because they worked and sometimes paid with their lives for the social and political changes guaranteeing the common well-being. They died so that we could live, and we are dying without living. These men and women were free. Freedom acts. Freedom is not given; it is fought for. Freedom is the refusal to suffer. Freedom must be put to the test, proven, and felt. Freedom submits the individual to the test of truth and adversity by requiring her to come out of herself. Freedom requires the subject to draw a clear and visible line between the apparent finitude of her condition and the infinitude of her potential. Freedom says "no" to what is and works to bring forth what is not yet. Freedom is the ultimate motor of history.

"You either have to be part of the solution, or you're going to be part of the problem," said Eldridge Cleaver.[19] For those who place hope in the return of a messiah, the poet June Jordan responds, "We are the ones we have been waiting for."[20] Whether a result of our success or our failures, Africa is us. Whether in Douala, Paris, or New York, the continent will be what we make of it. *"On va faire comment?"* Instead of dragging our existence like a millstone, instead of carrying our destiny like cursed fetuses that we wish to abort, what if we finally took possession of them? Could we invest the prophetic energy of survival in the *res publica*?

In the beginning, our countries came into existence accidentally. Today, we must imagine living together in spaces whose outlines we did not draw. Spaces that we are condemned to inhabit, to share, and to enrich. Therefore, we must confer them with a range of meanings and perspectives. Situations of scarcity should not mutilate our being in the world nor shut the door to the future, but cause a crisis of conscience.[21] The factual truth of our condition will not be able to impede the creation of tactics of civic engagement. Couldn't it contribute to an ethic of self-guaranteeing a society that raises people up rather than depreciating them?

Hope stands on a mountain of corpses. Our History bears witness to the irreversibility of moving forward. The difficulties that we are facing at the present time annihilate the efforts accomplished by our enslaved and colonized ancestors. They fought for freedom because they were oppressed. They built an edifying community, affirmed caring for the self and others, chose armed or civic struggle. Today, those who were born "free" live "in chains." Shall we continue to be subjected to History or make it come about? Shall we create our world or endure it like a curse? Shall we see existence as a merciless punishment or express the intentionality of an acting conscience? We must accept the consequences of our choices. To want and to be able is to obey. According to Nietzsche, a "man who wills commands something within himself that renders obedience."[22] Civic will is not a cancerous tumor to remove nor a gangrenous leg to amputate. A seed of becoming planted in the hard earth, it must be watered with the tears of hope, devotion, courage, and obstinacy. We will harvest, I am convinced, the fruits of a hard labor that will benefit posterity.

NOTES

1. Pierre Bourdieu, *Ce que parler veut dire*, Paris, Fayard, 1982, p. 14.
2. According to the philosopher Louis Althusser, this oppressive apparatus includes the government, the police, the courts, and prisons.
3. Achille Mbembe, *De la postcolonie. Essai sur l'imagination politique dans l'Afrique contemporaine*, Paris, Karthala, 2000.
4. Joe La Conscience is a Cameroonian artist who denounced the reconsideration of term limits of the presidency. He also tried to collect signatures for a memorandum against the modification of the constitution. For this, he was condemned to six months of prison.
5. A discursive act through which the speaker presents an image of herself.
6. Elias Kifon Bongmba analyzes the African crisis according to four parameters: the privatization of power, the pauperization of the state, the wasteful state, and the proliferation of violence. *The Dialectics of Transformation in Africa*, New York, Palgrave Macmillan, 2006.
7. I am referring here to Michel Foucault's idea. Instead of "referring to a theory of the subject [we must] analyze the different forms by which the individual is led to constitute himself as a subject. [Operating] a displacement, moving from the question of the subject to the analysis of forms of subjectivization, through techniques/technologies of the relationship to self [. . .] through what we could call a pragmatics of the self." *Gouvernement de soi et des autres*, Paris, Gallimard, Éditions du Seuil, 2008, p. 6–7.
8. On September 13th, 1958, Ruben Um Nyobe, a nationalist militant and the Secretary-General of the Union of the Peoples of Cameroon (UPC) was killed by colonial troops.
9. Célestin Monga, *Nihilisme et Négritude*, Paris, Presses universitaires de France, 2009, p. 44.
10. Paget Henry, "Africana Phenomenology: Its Philosophical Implications," *Worlds & Knowledge Otherwise*, 2006.
11. During a talk presented at the conference on African Literature in April 2009 in Burlington, Vermont, Professor Cilas Kemedjio mentioned this concept that I borrow here.
12. A play on words, "commemoration" is divided into the words *"comme-mes-morts-action,"* literally "like-my-dead-action." The act of commemoration is not about worshipping the dead, but acting in accordance with their legacy.
13. Motorcycle taxis.
14. Hand-cart operators.
15. Jean-Godefroy Bidima, *La Philosophie négro-africaine*, p. 103.
16. Paul Ricœur, *Soi-même comme un autre*, p. 370–371.
17. Frantz Fanon, *Pour la révolution africaine*, Paris, Éditions La Découverte/Poche, p. 60.
18. Hannah Arendt, *Qu'est-ce que la philosophie de l'existence*, Paris, Éditions Payot et Rivages, p. 73–74.
19. *Eldridge Cleaver: Post-Prison Writings and Speeches*, edited by Robert Scheer, New York, Random House, p. 130.
20. June Jordan, *Directed by Desire*, p. 279.
21. I use the term "crisis" in reference to a set of general and local reactions that suggest a decisive change in the organization of our societies. I consider situations that are troubled due to the interruption of social, political, economic, and cultural equilibrium as ones that the individual is condemned to reestablish. I also think of the vocabulary of theater in which the crisis is the knot of dramatic action, characterized by intense conflict between the passions that leads to the denouement.
22. Friedrich Nietzsche, *Par-dela bien et mal*, Paris, Flammarion, "GF," 2000, p. 66.

Chapter Nine

Coda

I find myself suddenly in a world in which things do evil; a world in which I am summoned into battle; a world in which it is always a question of annihilation or triumph.
—Frantz Fanon

You could not accept this burden. You could not accept this past as your present and much less your future.
—James Baldwin

Africans and people of African descent have made their entry into a global world through an experience rooted in loss and mourning. Still, this double negative does not prevent us from affirming the absolute superiority of life. It is not a question of putting on the shroud of suffering to glorify pain or to drown in its reflection, but to resituate our suffering by forging a relationship with the Other and with the self. Delving into suffering reveals that this experience can create a common humanity. Those who are subjected to suffering and those who inflict it are inseparable. To suffer is to have both the victim and the tormentor within oneself. According to the choreographer Heddy Maalem, pain is music. It has movement. It swirls around inside us. Animal, instinctive, rebellious against all conciliations, definitively twisted, in the grey, torn apart, offsides, at the edge of the black and white checkerboard spattered with the blood of certainty. Even in power relations, fragility brings people together. Fragility strengthens compassion and empathy. What do you feel when you hear a baby cry? When you witness a car accident? When you see the distress of a grief-stricken woman who has lost her husband, her son, or her daughter in a terrorist attack? When you hear the resounding tears of the Palestinians? Why did Jean-Marie Colombani write in an editorial in *Le Monde* on September 13th, 2001: "We are all

71

Americans"? What about the journalist of the *New York Times* who affirmed after the earthquake of January 1st, 2010: "We are all Haitians"? What do we do with our pain? With the Other's pain? Jesus Christ, Mahatma Gandhi, Malcolm X, Martin Luther King Jr., John F. Kennedy, Che Guevara, Um Nyobe, Patrice Lumumba, Steve Biko, Amilcar Cabral: murdered. Why does the violent end of certain religious or historical figures become a testament to love and peace that posterity holds on to? Why do we feel rage or powerlessness when suffering manifests itself in natural disasters, violence, poverty, sickness, hate of the Other, indifference, and devalued death?

In situations of war and oppression, those who administer suffering can use alcohol, drugs, and rationalize the irrational to kill that which demands human beings to recognize themselves in the Other. Unless we consciously or unconsciously proceed with this mutilation of the soul, by looking at the one who is experiencing pain, we sustain an intimate injury that is more or less (un)bearable. The transversality of the gaze ties the external image with the internal image. I associate what I observe with what I feel while observing. The transversality of the gaze returns us to our own vulnerability. It pushes us to distress, to compassion, or to action, sometimes all three at the same time. It suffices to notice the wave of solidarity that follows national disasters or terrorist attacks. In periods of endless violence, human beings are capable of the worst but also of the best. In the end, I wonder why and how we are able, in particular circumstances, to resist our weaknesses. How do we rebuild ourselves from what has been destroyed? What do we do with peoples who are not able to do so? What don't they succeed? How do destruction and relation modulate the music of existence?

In light of current events, I also wonder about the banalization of suffering. Observed from afar, it is apprehended from a place of detachment or finds itself exploited in a new economy of Western self-esteem that pours itself out in a praxis of humanitarianism in which charity is a substitute for political responsibility. When all forms of revolt have been neutralized by the soldiery of democracies that stink of dictatorship, the ubiquity of suffering creates a habituation to adversity. With an intrepid fatalism, the practice of existence gives birth to mechanisms of self-defense in which heroism and defeatism blend. What are we to make of these existential discontinuities? Why and how can we easily move from a sudden burst of solidarity in reaction to a tragedy to constant disinterest in a routine that incinerates life? Wouldn't it be possible to decode in the heart of the human experience an unlimited potential defined by truth, justice, forgiveness, peace, and love? Shouldn't we cultivate, with Franklin Nyamsi, a "globalization of destinies that will allow for a concrete and empathetic realization of the impact of the dramas of every society in the world on all the others"?[1]

I would like to say to Africans and to people of African descent that in many respects our lives are not easy. However, they remain less difficult than those of our ancestors who accomplished so much with so little. Trapped in the womb of death, forced to drink the *vie-nègre* of their condition,[2] confronted by distressed and confined wandering, those who were Black as night raised fortresses of hope with nothing, out of nothing. Do you sometimes think about the indigo experience of those who captured the Absurd with the lasso of resilience? Do you ever imagine the rhythmic cries of a black sun dressed in scrap iron?

The slave hangs on to the barbed asperities of metallic life, imploring the gods that entrusted her to senselessness. *Nyambé.*[3] *Orishas.*[4] *Shango.*[5] *Allah. Why have you forsaken me?*

Hotep.[6] *Ashe.*[7] *Heri.*[8] Have you seen the extinguished smile of the woman with burnt skin? She showers with tenderness the progeny of those who covered her with sadness. Held to her right breast, a blond head feeds greedily. What has become of her children? Have you heard the strangled moan of the man condemned to penal servitude, humiliated in front of his own, prisoner on the ancestral ground that became the private property of the newcomer? Do you think about those who died so that we can live?

Sa nou pa wé no[9] . . . "The dead are not dead." Crouched in the invisible spheres, eyes gorged with hope, they continue to cling to life. *Melancholia africana* . . . exhausted souls pour azure adagios in the amphora of soundless agony. Posterity must carry on the marathon of existence. The ancestors delivered them. They must now free themselves.

> *You say life's been hard on you*
> *Well brother I got news; it's hard on me too*
>
> *We seem to face*
> *The same old issues*
>
> *Some are just surface*
> *Some are deep*
> *Some deep down in the tissue*
>
> *And I know slavery has played its part, word*
> *Being separated and subjugated*
>
> *That passes*
> *to the brain of our child*
>
> *So I want to step off what was*
> *And start with the right now*
>
> *You say "the world just don't understand"*
> *But I ain't the world my love*
> *I'm your woman*

And I know how deep it really goes
Trying to tread on a dream
When the water feels low

Oh, if our ancestors could walk in the dark
Barefoot, afraid in the dark, for miles and miles,
And miles and miles and miles and miles and miles.

I know we can do this,
come on let's start. [10]

NOTES

1. Franklin Nyamsi, *Critique de la tragédie kamerunaise*, Paris, L'Harmattan, 2014, p. 90.
2. La "vie-nègre," literally, "negro life," which sounds like "vinegar" in French.
3. "God," in the Douala language.
4. The Orishas are the divinities of Santería. This religion, present in the Caribbean, syncretizes Catholicism and Yoruba spirituality.
5. Shango is the Orisha of war, thunder, and fire.
6. In Ancient Egypt, Hotep is the god of offerings. His name means "to be in peace, satisfied."
7. "So be it," in Yoruba.
8. "Goodness," in Swahili.
9. "The invisibles," in Haitian Creole.
10. Extract of the poem "Ain't A Ceiling," by Jill Scott, Def Jam Poetry, Season 6. https://www.youtube.com/watch?v=Fq3vxvaq484.

Epilogue

Interview with Nathalie Etoke on *Melancholia Africana: The Indispensable Overcoming of the Black Condition*, conducted by LaRose T. Parris

LaRose T. Parris: *Melancholia Africana*'s opening sentence announces a tension between phenomenological reality and linguistic expression when you explain that we inhabit a world "where thought closes itself in language that strives to erase the sensitivity of existence." Yet, as your text eloquently shows, African and African diasporic peoples' experience of anti-Black racism has generated a rich array of creative works that render the avowedly inexpressible aspects of mourning and loss poignantly clear. Given this tension between the phenomenological and expressive dimensions of human reality, what ideological and discursive role do you envision *Melancholia Africana* playing within the realm of Africana letters?

Nathalie Etoke: To be honest, when I wrote this book nine years ago, I did not envision that it would play any ideological or discursive role in the realm of Africana letters. All I wanted to do at the time was to offer a political, historical, cultural, philosophical, and creative reflection on the existence of continental and diasporic Africans. I strove to develop a poetic of consciousness that stems from loss, mourning, and survival in the context of imperialism, white supremacy, anti-Black racism, and the legacy of slavery and colonization.

I also believe that examining loss, mourning, and survival allowed me to address facticity, being, and becoming in a responsible manner. Beyond territorial expropriation and the pain inflicted upon the body and the soul, the violence that seals the encounter with the "other" annihilates an age-old cycle of life. In the wake of this annihilation, continental and diasporic Africans have striven to reconcile that which has been destroyed with what has been newly introduced. Looking at the ways in which their survival depends on their capacity to negotiate the inherent tension of their historical becoming is at the core of my thought. Consequently, problematizing the paradigm of victimhood as it pertains to people of African descent became somewhat of an obsession. I wanted to elaborate a discourse that shows people of African descent as victims who refuse to be victimized and that discourse focuses on their ability to recognize themselves as human beings, exercising their agency in the midst of their oppression. Nine years after the French publication and in thinking about the world of Africana letters, I hope that *Melancholia Africana* will be a contribution to the theorizing of "freedom from bondage" and "freedom in bondage"[1] or part of the relentless exploration of human possibilities in a dehumanizing world.

Parris: The concept of *for/giving*, as that which "is obtained through giving," is introduced as a vital requisite for moving past the oppression and dehumanization of anti-Black racism *and* the dependency/victimization complex that haunts many African and African diasporic peoples. While *for/giving* illuminates the empathetic reciprocity that lies at the heart of all genuinely compassionate human interactions, because of the normalization of white supremacy and anti-Black violence, it seems that *for/giving* may be unattainable for many whites. In your view, what educational, socio-political, and cultural steps need to be taken to awaken whites to the necessity and possibility of *for/giving*?

Etoke: Maybe I am somewhat pessimistic or too realistic about this issue. When I think about *for/giving*, it is both a two-way and a one-way street. In order for it to be a two-way street, we need reciprocity. As stated in the book, the oppressor must acknowledge in real, concrete terms that terrible harm has been done while the oppressed must accept her public acknowledgement of historical wrongs. From political and institutional standpoints, policies targeting historically oppressed people must be implemented, or there should be a commitment to reparation, social justice, equality, and freedom for all. However, I have lived long enough to see that this approach to *for/giving* is an endless struggle. I also believe that, at the end of the day, whites are the only people who can do what it takes to awaken themselves to the necessity and possibility of *for/giving*. We can't do that for them. When I teach courses that address the issue that you raise here, I still have to face resistance from some white students, but not all. Since I present the same material to the class, why is it that some awaken to the necessity and the possibility of *for/giving* while others do not? Is it about the education that many other educators like yourself and I can provide, or is it primarily about the choices that whites choose or choose not to make? We are still paying the price of their bad faith. To paraphrase Lewis Gordon, I would say that this bad faith creates a society where whites do not act as responsible agents or even feel the urge to do so. But, ultimately, it is their responsibility.

Given that, the question is what do *we* do as diasporic and continental Africans, when facing the denial of racism and white supremacy? We still have a life to live and a destiny to fulfill. Reflecting back on the history of Black freedom, I realized that nothing was ever given. Everything was born out of a struggle and that is still the case. Accordingly, no matter how daunting Black existence is, people of African descent must continue to develop creative agency that disrupts the power structure and the normalization of white supremacy. The West is still unable to face the history of oppression it created and perpetuates. At some level I agree with you that *for/giving* may be unattainable for whites. However, my approach to *for/giving* is an offering, not a demand. I also do not want to mystify racial identity because I strongly believe that, in spite of oppression and determinism, for better or worse, human beings are who they choose to be. All we have is each other. Therefore, if those who call themselves white, the inheritors of white supremacy, choose to reject that identity by facing the history that manufactured it and in which we are still entrapped, there is hope for *for/giveness*. It is white people's responsibility, not mine or yours. However, if they reject *for/giveness*, we still have a life to live. If we exhaust our energy by waking them up to the possibility of *for/giving*, we are in some respects reinforcing white power and surrendering our ability to create the world in which we wish to live.

Educational, socio-political, and cultural steps have been taken for decades. Yes, there is room for improvement, but I have nothing original to offer on the specifics of how to proceed. As an educator, I am constantly reminded that providing knowledge about racism or raising awareness of racism and issues that pertain to *for/giveness* does not necessarily lead to action or conflict resolution.

Parris: Chapter 1's discussion of diasporic consciousness "introduce[s] inventiveness into the relationship with History, the self, and the Other" and "allows for the construction of a common memory that submits to historical and personal dissent." One may consider in the Black radical tradition one crucial aspect of historical and personal dissent related to the history of chattel slavery and systemic oppression. Central to Cedric Robinson's explanation of the Black radical tradition is the position that the ancestors resisted oppression in order to maintain "collective ontological totality,"[2] and that their victory could not be measured in traditional terms.

However, in *Melancholia Africana* you state that "the ancestors were defeated." At the same time, in the analysis of Negro spirituals you also underscore that "by singing their suffering, the slave refuses to submit to an everyday life that denies their humanity. This suffering expresses itself through a structure of desire whose deepest aspiration responds to a sole expectation: freedom." Since this opposition between material and ontological freedom is presented, how do you describe *Melancholia Africana*'s reimagining of the interrelationship between historical reality, the self, and the Other in relation to existential freedom and its political import for the Black radical tradition?

Etoke: For the sake of clarity, it is necessary to contextualize the quote about defeat. I wrote: "The ancestors were defeated. Before laying down arms, they often resisted. Many died in combat. Piled in the valley of the shadow of oblivion, their dry bones exhale life. Amassed in the blue cenotaph, the wandering souls of the underwater necropolis let out the rough groans of a voiceless heroism. In the face of defeat, there is often great courage." In chapter 5 of *The Ambiguous Adventure*, Senegalese writer Cheikh Hamidou Kane offers a fictitious account of the encounter between Africa and the West. He talks about "a great clamor." As she describes her father's resistance to oppression, The Most Royal Lady, one of the main characters, says: "He took his gun and followed by all the élite of the region, he flung himself upon the newcomers. His heart was intrepid, and to him the value of liberty was greater than life. Our grand-father and the élite of the country with him was defeated."[3] At the most fundamental level, my understanding of defeat in the context of *Melancholia Africana* refers to the tragic facts of African and Afro-Diasporic life and history: slavery, colonialism, violence, and their consequences in the *longue durée* of imperialism since 1492. However, if you look at the entire passage, while talking about defeat, I bring to the fore "a voiceless heroism" and life that emerges out of the worst of circumstances: death. That kind of heroism is voiceless because it does not fit the Western episteme. In the wake of the initial defeat against the West, continental and diasporic Africans strive to reconcile that which has been destroyed with what has been newly introduced.

To paraphrase Walter Mignolo, I would say that my approach to victory and defeat is grounded on "complementary dualities (and/and) rather than on dichotomies or contradictory dualities (either/or)."[4] The triumph of our ancestors was born on the site of disaster. Victory grew out of defeat. Following in the footsteps of Frantz Fanon, I must grapple with the fact that the Western forces of imperialism have imposed an existential deviation on us. Thus, the dialectics of victory and defeat, existential freedom and political freedom are central to my reflection on loss, mourning, and survival. Maintaining a "collective ontological totality" is a process that occurs in the womb of death—white supremacist society—which by definition is the matrix of Black ontological destruction. In "Lived Experience of the Black," the fifth chapter of *Black Skin, White Masks*, Fanon opens: "Dirty Nigger! Or simply, 'Look, a Negro!' I came into the world imbued with the will to find a meaning in things, my spirit filled with the desire to attain to the source of the world, and then I found that I was an object in the midst of other objects."[5] This objectification and epidermalization led to an ontological explosion of the self whose "*fragments* have been put together again by another self."[6] What breaks Black humanity makes it whole. In this context, defeat is the introductory stage of victory. Defeat is what the history and the legacy of white supremacy has done/does to people of African descent. Victory is rooted in a way of life in which "origins are for one part a matter of survival, in another part a battle against the forces of unhappiness, anxiety and desperation."[7] Victory is the constant commitment to struggle with the tension between domination and freedom; denunciation of a system of oppression and the assertion of agency. Victory is finding a way to be human in a dehumanizing white supremacist world. It is a never-ending struggle. . . . Victory is in the struggle itself.

Parris: *Melancholia Africana*'s discussion of colonial (mis)education's successful occlusion of the philosophical and political import of Aimé Césaire's works, *Cahier d'un retour au pays natal* and *Discours sur le colonialisme*, is highly effective in its portrayal of how we are systematically programmed to cultivate a deep understanding of the works of white European and American thinkers while viewing those of African and African diasporic peoples as inscrutable.

Quite interestingly, in your discussion of the futility of comparing the near African genocide resulting from Western chattel slavery and the Jewish holocaust, you do not cite Césaire's emphasis (in *Discours*) that the former offered both historical precedent and ideological justification for the latter. Given that most Western readers are not necessarily versed in this aspect of Césaire's anti-colonial discourse, how does your call for readers to remember that "Lady Day sings to words of Abel Meeropol" and "Anne Frank reads her diary to Emmett Till" address the historical erasure of Black suffering that Césaire decries?

Etoke: When I wrote the book, there was a lot of tension in France around "competitive memories" or "*concurrence des mémoires*." The Black comedian Dieudonné referred to the "Holocaust" as "memorial pornography." He asked why there was no memorial for victims of the slave trade. Because he was unable to obtain public funding for his movie on the "Code noir," he questioned why the French state supported more than 150 movies about the Holocaust. Dieudonné has a lot of followers who are Blacks and Arabs and working-class white French people. Although I empathize with his willingness to challenge the historical erasure of Black suffering, I disagree with his approach. I was deeply concerned about the polarization of racial groups that have been historically oppressed. In seeking legitimate recognition, they sometimes fall prey to a divisive ideology that prevents solidarity and meaningful alliances. I should have included both Césaire and Fanon in that conversation. As you rightly said, Césaire explains how Western chattel slavery offers both historical precedent and ideological rationalization for the Holocaust. And Fanon reminds us that: "When you hear anyone abuse the Jews, pay attention; he is talking about you."[8] Rather than comparing Black pain to Jewish pain in pursuit of state-bestowed recognition, I propose that we examine the limits and the dangers of competitive memory, which reproduce a hierarchy of suffering. Also, we should reflect on strategies that help us address the politics of recognition in a creative and disruptive manner.

Parris: History seems to occupy a contested discursive space in *Melancholia Africana.* On the one hand, readers are alerted to George Lamming's insightful remark that the European trade in African slaves created the first modern globalized economy and that "globalization fell in our laps several centuries ago when Europe landed on the continent." Yet, on the other hand, readers are admonished for mistakenly believing that raising the mainstream reading public's awareness of ancient and medieval Africa's contributions to Western civilization would somehow remedy racist thinking.

Since most Western readers (of all races) lack a basic understanding of how the European trade in African slaves transformed the world economy and that its ideological underpinnings necessitated an erasure of ancient African history, how should this crucial information be disseminated in order to address what you describe in the book's opening as the African and African diasporic life experience "rooted in suffering born of social, economic, cultural, and historical structures dominated by unequal power relations"?

Etoke: Fanon writes: "The discovery of the existence of a Negro civilization in the fifteenth century confers no patent of humanity on me. Like it or not, the past can in no way guide me in the present moment."[9] I agree and disagree with this statement. I believe that diasporic and continental Africans should first know their history for themselves, but not because they have something to prove to the West. From age three to age eighteen, I was educated in Cameroon, Africa. However, the education I received was rooted in the colonial legacy. I did not learn about the nationalist struggle, Ruben Um Nyobé, or colonial violence in school. My dad, who was eleven years old when Cameroon became independent, was my history teacher. He told me stories about how he walked over dead bodies on his way to school. He told me about public executions, etc. I grew up in a dictatorship which either erased or manipulated the country's history of resistance. When we talk about the erasure of Black history, I would like us to remember that you cannot erase something that does not exist. In the same vein, you cannot dehumanize that which is not human.

Do you remember the controversy surrounding a textbook that referred to enslaved Africans as "workers" rather than "slaves"? This situation occurred in Texas in 2015. You and I both know that this outrageous rewriting of history/erasing of Black oppression was not a mistake or due to a lack of information. Why would a major publisher frame the history of Black oppression in the broader narrative of immigration? A Black mother went online and exposed the textbook and the school.

Western (white) readers lack basic understanding of how the European trade in African slaves transformed the world economy because it solidifies white privilege and the white supremacist matrix of power. How is it that people know about the moon and the stars and still know nothing about the history of oppression that built Western wealth? How is it that in 2019, we still have to raise the mainstream reading public's awareness of ancient and medieval Africa's contribution's to global civilization? Is it just because the information is not being disseminated?

Minority readers are educated in a society that promotes the erasure of their history and their contributions to humanity. That's the rub. White readers are ignorant not because of the lack of information or possibilities to be educated on topics such as power, race, and imperialism. White supremacy shapes and controls the society in which we live by deliberately choosing to ignore the history of this country. It creates a system of reality that deludes and distracts white people from issues of power and social inequalities. But white supremacy is not an external supernatural force; it has to do with the choices that white people make to control all aspects of society—culture, politics, economy, education—in order to promote their racial superiority and maintain their privileges. To go back to your initial question, ignorance about African history and the contribution of people of African descent to the world is a form of bad faith or a denial and an evasion of responsibility. The lack of understanding is not only due to the lack of information or dissemination of that information. Even when the information is available, people do not necessarily act on what they know because it is risky: they will lose their privilege and have to address social justice and freedom for all. The question is, do they really want to do that?

Parris: Reminiscent of Du Bois's *The Souls of Black Folk*, *Melancholia Africana* presents a transdisciplinary analysis of anti-Black racism's ideological and structural formations, as well as an examination of African and African diasporic peoples' lived experience of anti-Black racism. Central to both *Souls* and *Melancholia Africana* are incisive readings of African diasporic music as creative articulations of spiritual transcendence and existential freedom. In fact, you state that "if diasporic consciousness were a musical genre, it would inevitably be jazz." In light of this Black existential aesthetic, if you were to take this comparison one step further, with what jazz classics or jazz artists would you equate the introduction, parts I and II, and the coda (itself a musical term) of *Melancholia Africana*?

Etoke: That's a very difficult question.

The jazz theme for the introduction would be "Crepuscule with Nellie" by Thelonious Monk[10] or "Medi I" by Mary Lou Williams[11]; for part I: "Search for the New Land" by Lee Morgan[12]; for part II: "Moanin" by Charles Mingus[13]; for the coda: "A Love Supreme, Part 1: Acknowledgement" by John Coltrane[14] or "Straight Ahead" by Abbey Lincoln.[15]

NOTES

1. James H. Cones, *The Spirituals and the Blues*, Maryknoll, NY, Orbis Books, p. 28.

2. Cedric Robinson, *Black Marxism: The Making of the Black Radical Tradition*, Chapel Hill, NC, University of North Carolina Press, 1983, p. 171.

3. Cheikh Hamidou Kane, *The Ambiguous Adventure*, translated by Katherine Woods, Brooklyn, NY, Melvin House Publishing, 1963, p. 33.

4. Walter Mignolo and Catherine E. Walsh, "The Invention of the Human and the Three Pillars of the Colonial Matrix of Power," in *On Decoloniality: Concepts, Analytics, Praxis*, Durham, NC, Duke University Press, 2018, p. 155.

5. Frantz Fanon, *Black Skin, White Masks*, New York, Grove Press, 1967, p. 109.

6. *Ibid.*

7. Lewis Gordon, "L'existence noire dans la philosophie de la culture," *Diogène* 235–236, July 2011, p. 143.

8. Fanon, *Black Skin, White Masks*, p. 122.

9. Fanon, *Black Skin, White Masks*, p. 225.

10. On *John Coltrane and Thelonious Monk Complete Studio Recordings*, Vintage Records, 2008.

11. On *Zoning*, Smithsonian Folkways, 1995.

12. On *Search For The New Land*, Blue Note, 2003.

13. On *Blues & Roots*, Atlantic Masters, 2008.

14. On *A Love Supreme*, Impulse/Verve, 2003.

15. On *Straight Ahead*, Candid, 1961.

Index

Absurd, the, 10, 15, 16, 31, 37, 50, 72
Africa; *passim*, but especially, ix, xiv, xx,
    1, 9, 11, 12n5, 15, 18, 37, 41, 42, 43,
    47, 56, 57, 68
African oral tradition, 40
Africans; *passim*, but especially, 24n24,
    35, 37, 39, 47, 62n11, 64, 71, 72, 75–81
African antiquity, xiii
African descent, people of, xxi, xxiin2,
    7–9, 19, 31, 39, 60, 71–72, 75, 77, 78,
    81
African diaspora; *passim*, but especially,
    3–4, 6
Afro-modernity, xii
AIDS (Acquired Immune Deficiency
    Syndrome), 47, 56
Ancestors, the, xi, xxi, 17, 21, 35, 37, 73,
    77–78
Ani, xiii
apartheid, 21, 23n11, 62n11
Appiah, K. Anthony, 1
Arabs, 79
Ashanti, 3–4

bad faith, xiii, 76–81
Baldwin, James, xx, xxiin3
Baluba, 3–4
Bamileke, 3–4, 7
Baraka, Amiri, 22n2
Benin, 44n1
Benjamin, Walter, xxi, xxiiin6, 35, 44n26

Bhabha, Homi, 62n17
Bidima, Jean-Godefroy, 44n25
Biko, Steve, 71
Blacks; *passim*, but especially, 3–8, 12n14,
    15, 20, 24n24, 24n26, 60, 62n11, 79; in
    France, 3
Black existential aesthetics, 22n2, 81–82
#BlackLivesMatter, ix, xiv
Blanchard, Terence, 40
blues (music), xiv, xx–xxi, xxiin5, 10, 15,
    16, 22n5, 32
body, the, xviii, xix, xxiiin7, 10, 44, 52, 75
Brown Jr., Oscar, 44n18
Buddhism, 64
Butler, Judith, 10, 13n21

Cabral, Amilcar, 71
Cameroon, 7, 37, 63–67, 80; state, 44n2
Cape Coast Castle, 44n1
Caribbean, 3, 4, 6–8, 12n14, 17–18, 25,
    74n4
Caribbean Philosophical Association, vii,
    87, 88
castration, x, 20, 59
Cazenave, Noël, ix
Charles-de-Gaulle University, 25
Colombani, Jean-Marie, 71
colonized, the; *passim*, but especially, xxi,
    10, 12n14, 24n24
color-blind, 4–5
Coltrane, John, 22n2, 40, 44n24, 82, 82n10

About the Author, Translator, and Contributors

Nathalie Etoke is Associate Professor of Francophone and Africana Studies at the Graduate Center, CUNY. Her articles have appeared in *Research in African Literatures, French Politics and Culture, Nouvelles Études Francophones, Présence Francophone, International Journal of Francophone Studies*, and *Journal of French and Francophone Philosophy*. She is the author of *L'Écriture du corps féminin dans la littérature de l'Afrique francophone au sud du Sahara* and of *Melancholia Africana l'indispensable dépassement de la condition noire*, which won the 2012 Frantz Fanon Prize from the Caribbean Philosophical Association. In 2011, she directed *Afro Diasporic French Identities*, a documentary film on race, identity, and citizenship in contemporary France.

Lewis R. Gordon co-edits Rowman & Littlefield International's Global Critical Caribbean Thought series. He is Professor of Philosophy at UCONN-Storrs; Honorary President of the Global Center for Advanced Studies; the 2018–2019 Boaventura de Sousa Santos Chair in Faculty of Economics of the University of Coimbra, Portugal; and Chair of Global Collaborations for the Caribbean Philosophical Association. His public Facebook page is https://www.facebook.com/LewisGordonPhilosopher/ and he is on Twitter @lewgord.

Bill Hamlett is a translator, researcher, and teacher of French. He holds master's degrees in French from Middlebury College and in Literary Theory from the École Normale Supérieure.

LaRose T. Parris is Associate Professor of English at LaGuardia Community College/CUNY. Her first book, *Being Apart: Theoretical and Existential Resistance in Africana Literature* (University of Virginia Press, 2015), was awarded the Nicolás Guillén Prize for Outstanding Book in Philosophical Literature by the Caribbean Philosophical Association in 2016. Her fiction and criticism have appeared in *Callaloo*, *Entre Letras*, the *Review of Education, Pedagogy, and Cultural Studies*, and the *Journal of Pan African Studies*.